KING EDWARD VII AND SOME
OTHER FIGURES

KING EDWARD VII
& SOME OTHER FIGURES

By

STUART R. J. ERSKINE
(The Hon. Ruaraidh Erskine of Marr)

Essay Index Reprint Series

BOOKS FOR LIBRARIES PRESS
FREEPORT, NEW YORK

First Published 1936
Reprinted in this Series 1966, 1969

STANDARD BOOK NUMBER:
8369-1331-0

LIBRARY OF CONGRESS CATALOG CARD NUMBER:
67-22092

PRINTED IN THE UNITED STATES OF AMERICA

l

CONTENTS

PREFACE

IN that part of his writings which is entitled *A Plan for a General History of Europe*, Bolingbroke, addressing the person to whom he was about to communicate his thoughts on this head, says:

You must not imagine that I am writing memoirs of myself. The subject is too slight to descend to posterity in any other manner than by that occasional mention which may be made of any little actor in the history of our age. Sylla, Caesar, and others of that rank were, while they lived, at the head of mankind; their story was in some sort the story of the world, and as such might very properly be transmitted under their names to future generations. But for those who have acted much inferior parts, if they publish the piece, and call it after their own names, they are impertinent: if they publish their own share they inform mankind by halves, and neither give much instruction nor create much attention.

As to this passage, I fear that if the sense of it were acted on generally, and with that strictness which my lord evidently intends, very little biography would be written, and still less autobiography composed. It might be said, and it would be said, too, plausibly enough, that though this should happen to us, yet no great harm would result. Bad biography, memoirs filled with trifles, trifling, and triflers, and autobiography that is ill conceived and worse written, abound among us to-day; and it is little suitable that shelves which should be reserved for better matter should instead groan beneath the weight of so much superfluous and 'impertinent' writing.

Still, it is plain that if none but great lives were written, and none but memoirs and autobiography of true moment composed, much that should be valuable to human experience would be lost, and a deal that might interest mankind would be missed. There are truths, most necessary to be learned, that lie midway 'twixt the two extremes of talent and mediocrity, of fame and obscurity; and, after all, is not the part of Time in this matter to precipitate to the bottom of the vase of letters the dross and the impurities that float at first on the surface? and thus are these waters cleared for posterity if not for us.

On the whole matter, then, I cannot help but think that though there is a deal of sense in what Lord Bolingbroke says, yet the law he gives is much too strict. The beasts of the field that, on a hot day, are so teased with flies that almost are they driven mad, must put up with the inconvenience, since they are not able to avert it; but our case, fortunately, is very different. We are at perfect liberty not to buy or borrow the indifferent literature glanced at: we need not trouble ourselves with it in any way, much less allow it to plague us, unless we so choose.

Biography and autobiography written with a psychological 'punch' are much in vogue nowadays. This is a tribute to Freud and Jung, and the Viennese pharmacopoeia generally. So far as this sign in a part of the firmament of letters is legible, and contains message of value, surely it is a good sign; but it is a bad sign when, as often happens, the author who writes 'psychology' writes, not it, but what he takes for it, or, very commonly, little but himself. The motives of men resemble a well without apparent bottom to it. A little way down this well, a trifle below the mouth of it, there is a fair visibility; but yet a little farther down, and all is dark; and here neither the apparatus of Freud, nor yet the machine of Jung, is of the smallest use to us, in order to enable us to see clearly at this, or any greater depth.

No man takes with him out of this world into the

next anything of that of which he was possessed whilst he was in it. The rich man, therefore, equally with him that is famous, leaves behind him when he dies, the first his riches, and the second whatever he may have amassed to himself by way of fame and honours in this life; and thus talent bent to either of the two ends glanced at would seem to be, *a priori*, wasted effort. Seneca has a good deal that is pregnant on this head, and Polybius, if my memory serves me well, has written in much the same sense.

I read somewhere lately that when it was suggested to Ibsen that the fame of his dramatic writings might not long survive the death of the author of them, he took umbrage at the notion, observing, with all the signs of extreme irritation in his countenance, that for his part he had not composed a single line, had he thought for a moment that he would not 'live,' in the extended sense sometimes given to this word. He appears not to have recollected the millions of the sons and daughters of Adam who died before our records begin, and among whom, presumably, were some at least of a talent considerable enough to be called great: nor yet the millions that existed, and have died, since these records began; but touching whom all surety is lost, though among these, as

among the others, were great men presumably.
Though a writer write for fame, or a painter
or a sculptor, a soldier or a statesman exert
his talent to the same end, yet he cannot
command it: nor is it reasonable in him to
expect it, or a sign of much intelligence in him
to desire it. To wish for ourselves 'immor-
tality' of fame on earth, what is this but mere
vanity? As to Ibsen, his memory is descending already the pit of oblivion: a century or
two hence and his remains will be but food
for worms in the shape of anthologists, compilers
of anecdotes, and vendors of literary curiosities.
I was in a London cemetery recently, and
observing about me grave after grave of un-
illustrious dead, 'After all,' I said to my com-
panion as we turned to leave the spot, 'is not
to survive in headstones fame enough for any
man, and the tomb the proper burial-place of
human vanity?'

There is a sort of greatness which descends
on us of itself and clothes us illustriously, as it
were; but there is also yet another kind, whose
spring or source is within ourselves. Doubtless
no man is great by reason alone of the greatness
of the undertaking to which he addresses himself. To be truly so under these conditions he
must have talent, commensurate in some sort

with the greatness of the object he thinks to com-
pass. Dante and his English imitator, Milton,
are examples of this order of greatness; and such
men as Napoleon, Alexander, and Caesar illustrate the other, and, I think, the inferior kind.
These men had vast talent certainly; but then
this it is, rather than the objects which they
set before them, that has rendered them illustrious, above the common. In any event, true
greatness is of so rare occurrence on earth that
whole centuries of time may go by, as they have
gone by, judging from history, without the
appearance of a single truly great man, though
to be sure each successive age may show a fair
sprinkling of very considerable minds.

The world is a stage, and the actors that
perform on it, each for a brief while, are like
to those that appear in the theatre proper,
being both great and small; and on both, too,
the 'little actors' are ever far more numerous
than the great. Some play big parts—whether
well or ill matters nothing here—but yet a
larger number minor ones; and, to complete
the parallel, there is as much and as great
variety of occasions, of opportunity, in the
enacting any one play that is designed for
the world-stage as there is in respect of the
longest and most finished piece that ever was

composed for the theatre, and performed on its boards.

Fame is fickle; neither is the measure of her awards always, or indeed very often, proportioned to the merit of the object of her flattering, though indiscriminating, attentions. Some that are famous in the vulgar eye deserve it not at all, most obviously; but, no less demonstrably, others there are who receive nothing of this sun, though they merit it, and on these, by consequence, it never sets. He to whom fame comes late, is more fortunate than he to whom it comes early, in life; and the reason of this is plain, since the first, amid all the temptations and distractions associated to fame, is apt to preserve the equanimity of his gifts, and thus prolong the life of his creative powers; but the second burns to distinguish himself farther, and yet more notably, and so is led to push his talent unduly, and thus (where this occurs) he undoes both it and himself. Fame has a trump; but sometimes the notes that issue from it are discordant enough: they who make bold to seize it, and blow it in their own behalf, seldom make tolerable music of it. There are qualities of human fame, as there are qualities of human greatness. Let us then divide the former into fame that is

intermittent, and fame that is continuous, by
nature; but, be it continuous or be it intermittent by nature, I hold that to speak of fame
as 'imperishable,' or of this or that memory as
'immortal,' is contrary to the law of God and
nature, and therefore bagatelle.

I set Gladstone second in my gallery of portraits, not because I have a particular regard
for his memory, esteem of his parts, or admiration of his achievements; but because I think
that he had, perhaps, some greatness in him;
though this I cannot allow (in a like degree at
least) to any of the others whose sketches here
appear; and also because his name happens to
figure second on the list of subjects with whom
I am to deal in this little work. But all have
been chosen in order to illustrate some one
aspect or other, or phase or point or quality,
of the different forms that human fame is apt
to take among us.

The common humour of writers as to readers
is that the first seek to constrain opinion as
they imagine it in the second, in the seeking
which they sometimes discover a deal of special
pleading, and behave themselves in print as
though they dreaded nothing more on earth
than that their readers should think and judge
differently from themselves. This little book

contains, I hope, none of this gross humour: if any cap fits, let him whose head it fits wear it; but as to the rest, far be it from me to seek to constrain opinion concerning human fame, or indeed regarding any other topic touched in the course of the present writing.

R. E. of M.

January 1936.

CHAPTER I

MARSIGLIO, who wrote fairly early in favour of government by a democracy, allows that 'perhaps a kingly rule is best,' since, of all the different forms of government, monarchy is apt to be the stablest. England is a monarchy; but then to this description of it we must add the epithet 'constitutional,' which means in effect that, in the last resort, the supreme power rests with the people, and not with the Crown, which must bend to this will, or run the hazards of defying it, as often as the people and the prince come to quarrel with one another, or take divergent views as to important matters of state.

Still, though the English is what is styled a limited monarchy, and the people the ultimate court of appeal and seat of authority of it, yet it is plain that, by virtue of this very description of it, the sovereign is entitled to a very high place in the constitution, so considerable indeed that it would be true to say that England is primarily a monarchy, having tacked on to it as it were this other provision of a limitation of power originating in the people, and belonging to it by indefeasible right. If, then, this conception of the nature of English monarchy be allowed — and for my part I venture to say that I see nothing in history or yet in reason to controvert, much less discount it—it should follow, I suppose, that, so far as the prince is concerned, his chief business and principal employment are, so to reign as to avoid all occasion of disagreement, of serious dispute, with the people, in order that the essential quality of the English system of rule (which is surely monarchy) may be maintained, and the Crown be active in government within the limits of the province which usage and the ingenuity of the jurists agree in assigning to it.

No doubt, the fact that the English is not a written, but a consuetudinary, constitution is a difficulty, in the sovereign's point of view at least. For though he may know for sure, in some particular case, where his right to rule begins, yet it by no means follows from hence that, in the same case, he may know with a like degree of certainty where precisely, or even contingently, the same right ends; and neither usage nor yet the jurists may be able to help him to resolve the problem.

The situation of the reigning prince in a

government such as appertains to the English is therefore apt to be an extremely difficult one, since it demands on the part of the ruler much talent, much wisdom and learning, and other very considerable gifts and virtues, not only so that he may maintain the Crown with credit, but also that he may know when and where to press its rights in respect to conjunctures and passages of politics in regard to which no positive guidance for him, drawn from the past, exists, and in respect to which too little, or too much, interference on his part may injure the Crown's interest, or even bring it into collision with its ultimate lord and master, the people. Constitutionally considered, the whole of the late Queen Victoria's reign was spent in a series of 'engagements' such as these remarks suggest; and if she had not talent, or help enough at the time, to enable her, as monarch, to bridge with success all the difficulties of this nature that befell her, some of them at least she so managed, and she deserves, I think, much credit for it, notwithstanding that in her day the power and authority of the Crown, as an integral part of the English political constitution, declined much and visibly.

In any historical comparison drawn between the family of Scotland on one hand and that of Hanover on the other, with a view to determining their respective merits as rulers of England, it should be recollected (and the weight that is due to this recollection given to it) that while the former reigned as unlimited, the part of the latter was to rule as limited, monarchs. It might be, and no doubt it so happened, that, after the Civil War, some limitation of political power, some pruning of the royal prerogative, was imposed on the Crown, if not positively by statute at least tacitly by reason of the rebellion glanced at; but till the revolution of the year 1688 came about, and the settlement of the Crown which followed it then, and the later one, were made, the authority of the sovereign in England was practically boundless, theoretically, if not substantially and positively, unlimited.

But very different was the situation of the Georges, who were invited, and came hither, under the wing of a triumphant political faction, the Whigs, and under these auspices these kings succeeded not to a full, but to a semi-deflated, constitution. The first two Georges were little better than creatures or puppets of the party that had brought the family in; but it happened that the third of the name had superior stuff in him, or came early under the influence of

some who, deploring the sinking state of the
English Crown, were resolved to make an effort
in order to stay its downward course. In any
event, no matter whether or no George III
resented the dictatorship of his family by the
Whigs, or was inspired to action by some more
respectable motive, what happened was that he
declared the Whig rule of the Crown, that is,
that of the families that regarded the Court
as their principal pocket-borough, at an end:
the throne recovered somewhat of its lost
prestige, and the sovereign some at least of
his former power to take an active visible part
in government.

The ascribing to the passage of the first
Reform Bill a threefold effect in the shape of the
disappearance of the remnants of the political
power of the Crown, the extinction of the
influence of the great Whig families in politics,
and the total disruption of the old Tory party,
would be, in part at least, a true ascription,
though, with regard to the first point, too
sweeping a deduction perhaps from the event
mentioned. It was said by some not long ago,
and has been a good deal echoed by others
since, that Queen Victoria exerted her principal influence in foreign affairs; and though
undoubtedly her power in this particular

province was very considerable, yet it should be remembered that, owing to the constitution of the different continental monarchies at the time, it was more easy for her to exert her influence with success outside her realm than within it; and, this being so, for my part I think that what merit she had as a ruler, and what influence she exerted as such, belongs more properly, and more immediately, to her domestic, rather than to her foreign, policy. Some of the administrations that were called to power by the popular voice in her day were extremely distasteful to her; and had she felt that the authority of the Crown was sufficient to it, or at least that she might well rid herself of them at no greater expense to the sovereign than a few murmurs in inconsiderable places, she had doubtless consulted her wishes by dismissing or refusing them office. However, as events fell out, it happened that her boldest and greatest stroke in behalf of the decaying prerogative of the Crown in government was to dismiss a minister: the action was a good deal questioned, and in some quarters sharply criticized, at the time; but the queen and her husband remained unmoved; and by this instance, if not by others of a like nature that I could cite, she showed the world that though in England the institution itself of monarchy might be in decay, yet the power and authority of the Crown, as touching its participation in the actual process of government, were by no means entirely at an end. The same instance, conjoined with the cognate, if lesser, examples that might be cited, discovers sufficiently the power and authority of the Crown in those days, and, at the same time, the political status of it, relatively to these. Perhaps the queen's greatest monument and title to respectful memory is that though she knew that the monarchy in England was an expiring institution, yet she, in these so difficult and discouraging circumstances, strove her utmost, bent all her talent, in order to postpone and ease, as far as might be, its days of decline.

It is advanced by some, indeed it is said by many, nowadays, that what the institution of monarchy lost in, England by way of political power has since been recovered to it, though in a different way, that is, through the channel of 'social prestige,' and they who hold this language speak of 'social prestige' much as though it were a kind of lesser beatitude, and, farther, as though it were in some sort an integral formal part of the English political constitution. That this, or indeed any other,

Crown should be popular with the multitude,
and that its social influence should be widely
diffused, and of the first quality and importance: these ends, no doubt, are well enough;
still, neither one nor the other of them has
any apparent connection with the solemn purpose for which the English monarchy, like
others, was, if not instituted, yet re-established
at least; which it discharged, more or less ably,
more or less conscientiously, through a long
course of history — that is to say the sharing,
in a direct and overt manner, in the business
of the civil government of the country.   There
are diseases that cause in some that fall victims
to them an air or appearance (which by reason
of the very nature of things cannot but be very
misleading) of health and general well-being;
just as there are herbs, and even trees, that, in
decay, put forth blossom more beautiful than
any which they showed before they were
stricken.   Polybius, surveying—shortly before
they fell—the republican institutions of the
Roman people, thought them perfect; but a
jurist who should be similarly employed to-
day with regard to the monarchial institutions
of the English people, might well be excused
if he thought them, on an examination of them,
in a very unhealthy state.   In fine, he who should

succeed in imagining to himself a ship that is all figurehead, and thus destitute of rudder, might well see in this strange object of the deep a perfect type of the English monarchy as it exists to-day.

Referring in one of his letters on the *Use and Study of History* to the education of princes, Bolingbroke says that this is 'generally bad'; and, for an example, he cites that of Louis XIV, who, he says, 'jested sometimes on his own ignorance,' though he allows freely enough that, thanks to the long instruction the king received at the hands of Mazarin, this great defect in him was less injurious to the royal interests than it had been, had not the states-man named 'initiated him betimes in the mysteries of his policy.' Why the education of princes should be more often bad than good is not easy to determine, save perhaps on the presumption that as more dull and mediocre human nature is born into this world than talent, so is this apt to appear as well in high places as in low. Certainly our immediate ancestors were used to take immense pains with the education of their princes. They dosed them regularly and repeatedly with such works as those of Fénelon and De Commines, with the Florentine histories and philosophy; and

Plutarch, whose forty-six portraits of great men, and other writings of a biographical nature, they esteemed very highly, as means to educational ends—these also they applied, and reapplied with a zeal and industry that were little short of extraordinary; so that the conclusion to which one is obliged, on a review of the whole matter, is, that if on the thrones of former times were monarchs whose education as such was demonstrably defective, this happened, not for want of means and endeavours to bring them to some better shape in this regard, but because these princes themselves lacked in themselves the power, the will, the application, and the disposition which were necessary in order to enable them to profit by the instruction so diligently imparted to them by pastors and masters. All this passion—for such it really was—for education in princes occurred after the resurrection of letters happened. Before the event I speak of came to pass, the princes of the West were suffered to run wild in their youth, devoting themselves to the profession of arms, to hunting, and, in their leisure hours, to gross amours and ignoble philanderings with the women of their courts, and those of others, without thought or heed on their part as to letters and education, save to despise both very heartily; as Francis I observed, acutely enough, on one occasion to Budé, who was his principal agent in his endeavours to bring his people, and particularly the nobles, to better manners, and to some understanding of the importance and advantage to them, and others, of politeness of conduct, and a good education. But though the judgment of Francis with regard to his contemporaries, and most of his predecessors, of France, and the West generally, was true and just enough, yet he seems to have forgot, or if he did not forget, would appear to have been ignorant of, the early example of the Celts of Gaul and the British Isles, who, among themselves, entertained the most liberal notions touching education, which they regarded, not as did the rulers of feudal Europe generally, that is to say as a sort of ecclesiastical preserve, but as a good fit for all, and therefore meet to be given to as many as called for it, and especially to ruling princes and other civil magistrates. By virtue and by reason of all which, the Celts are much distinguished in history, if not in the common repute, since, after the disappearance of the Roman power, they were by far the most civilized of all the different peoples of the West.

With the education of the prince who

became afterwards Edward VII of England, the greatest pains were taken and the utmost care was used. 'From his birth,' says Sir Sidney Lee, in his account of the life of the late king, 'his father thought to dedicate him apart to his inherited mission,' which means in effect that the child was but a few years out of the cradle when his parents came to sit in solemn council on the important matter of his future in the schools.

There is a Gaelic saying to the effect that the hills that lie farthest from us seem ever the bluest of all. One sees, and hears, nowadays, education attacked; because they who object to it think it not 'practical' enough, their notion being, apparently, that were this mill employed to grind out craftsmen, mechanics, and 'men of business' generally, its present reproach in the eyes of these critics, that it is medieval in form as in spirit, and so produces nothing but scholars (who are thus presumed to have no part to play in the modern world), would be taken from it, and that, by consequence, all might yet be well with mankind; and thus it happens that, in this matter as in many others that concern the well-being of society in general, the prick or goad of theory is employed in order to stir up the squirrel (which in captivity is the true type and emblem of man) to revolve, and to continue to revolve, the wheel of his cage.

But, no matter what defects might be in the general plan of the prince's education, no one surely should have the front to say that it was not 'practical,' having regard to the end or ends to which it was designed, and the quality and the political status of the person to whom all this *ad hoc* instruction was applied. For my part I venture to think that it was too 'practical' by half, and consequently that it had been all ways better, more suited to the object of it at least, had there been about it much less buckram and pipeclay, as it were, than was the case—more humanism, and greater elasticity of view: in fine, less 'technology,' and more of nature's easy and indulgent ways.

I have heard it said, and I think the anecdote is related by Sir Sidney Lee in his *Life* of King Edward, that when the prince consort, the queen, and Stockmar were busy together laying the plan of the boy's education, they, or at least one of the three, were warned by Lord Melbourne not to make the jacket too strait, nor yet to trust to it too much; for, says he in effect—the exact words he used on this occasion I disremember at the moment

—education should be proportioned to the subject's understanding; and though it may, and should, improve nature, yet it is powerless (said he) to change it. However, the three drove on with the business they had in hand like a ship before the wind, so that happened on this occasion which is prone to happen in similar circumstances, namely, that the words of warning and wisdom uttered by a master-mariner, a captain of the seas of worldly experience, fell all unheeded — worked no effect whatever.

To cavil at foreign nations and peoples, to harbour prejudice against them, merely because they may happen to have modes of thought, manners and customs, that differ considerably from those which we ourselves entertain, and to which we are accustomed and as firmly attached, is conduct unworthy of a wise man. Still, to object to the kind of education planned by his parents and Stockmar in behalf of the heir to the English throne, on the ground that it was altogether too Germanic by nature, seems to me reasonable enough. The German is too apt to propose 'according to plan'; and then when the will of God directly, or some permitted action on the part of some one or more of His creatures, opposes this plan, and brings it to naught, but rarely does it seem to occur to him that himself it is and his plan that are at fault, and not the external cause or causes of its undoing. In any event, the nature of the German genius is such that, being given to 'plan,' it is all too apt to plan without due regard to circumstance, to contingencies, to the latent forces and potentialities of particular men and situations of affairs; and above all, perhaps, to the tendency of natures and things in general to turn out differently to what is expected of them at first, and desired of them, too, very often, most devoutly. The conduct of the Empress Frederick in Germany, after the death of her husband, and the procedure in England of Victoria, Albert, and Stockmar, after they were come together to plan the prince's education, are circumstances formed to remind us that after all there may well be something in the Nordic theory besides false ethnology, and chronology as doubtful.

Apparently the heir to the Crown was presumed by his parents to love books even from his cradle, and to delight in learning whilst he was yet in arms; but it happened that the prince did neither, either at this period, or later when he was come to riper years. The grand presumption therefore was wrong: at least, if it were indulged by way of 'plan,' prudence counselled strongly that it should be held in abeyance, as it were, until such times as the prince himself might show unmistakably the natural cast and bent of his nature, which, as it happened, was in some sort 'mechanical,' but not, most certainly, at all 'bookish.'

Though a prince or other civil ruler be not 'bookish,' nor yet a votary of the Muses, nor temperamentally inclined to study, and the taking serious views of life, and his own part in it, yet, after all, such a one may well rise to eminence as a governor and leader of men— a thesis which I doubt not could be proved very easily, by examples drawn from history, if not from instances of a more immediate occurrence. But should it happen that the prince or other ruler has no natural liking for books, or genius for the learning that is to be got from some of them at least, it is plain that he must use some other study in order to fill the void that is in him, otherwise such chance as he may have to become eminent as a ruler will be but slender. Though he be not drawn to books, or attracted to learning, he must be ever acute to observe men, forward to learn from the lips of those who have knowledge of them the constitutions of states, and the

dispositions of the peoples that inhabit them;
how the different national interests lie, and in
what they consist, and so forth; and not only
must he seek all this information of such as
are best qualified, and the most advantageously
situated, in order to impart it to him, but also,
when at last he shall have acquired it, he must
ponder it at his leisure, and ever with the
utmost care and attention, to the end that
he too may fit himself to play his part as a
ruler with credit to himself, and with advantage
to his country. But unfortunately it happened
otherwise with regard to the prince who is
the subject of this sketch. He had no natural
liking, either for the society of those who were
qualified to give him the instruction which he
might have drawn, in part at least, from books,
had he cared to read them, or yet for the
withdrawing himself for a while from the
society of his companions, in order to meditate
in private, which, in the case of a prince who
aspires to shine in that particular quality, or in
that of one who is destined, as it were, to
the purple, is absolutely necessary, no matter
whether his choice of instructor for himself
be books or men or both, since no one can
hope with reason to profit to the full by instruction, whether oral or written by nature,

save he have time and opportunity enough in which to digest it properly.

The matter of the sort of company kept by the prince after he was come of age was, very naturally, one of much concern to the queen and her husband, who saw in it, I suppose, no bright augury as to the fulfilment of their common hopes in his regard, and, farther, proof in some sort perhaps, that, after all, their nice-laid plans with regard to their son's education had not worked entirely according to the design of them. It was this disposition on the part of the prince to seek his pleasures elsewhere than the queen expected, and thought suitable, and in forms and ways of which she no less strongly disapproved, as well for state as private reasons, that bred later a coolness between the two that endured all through the period of Her Majesty's retirement, after the death of the prince consort, and came not to an end till towards the close of the queen's life and reign. I have heard it said by some who were about the Court and person of the queen at the time, and who had good and sufficient opportunities of observing her, that though it may well have been some punctilio of respect and affection on her part touching the memory of her late husband, the prince consort, that prevented her in her later years from declaring her and his mistake with respect to the manner of the prince's education; yet I have heard it said that before she came to die she seemed to be reconciled in some sort to the great difference, in point of temper, and ways, habits, aims, and character that then existed, and had always existed, between her idea of an heir to the English throne and Prince Albert Edward, her son. So the tale goes that the years and disappointments and misfortunes had brought the queen phlegm, if not philosophy enough, to put up with, and even on occasions to seem pleased with that which, in the same respect, was now become in a manner unimprovable.

Tradition among crowned heads, as the same in less exalted quarters, is apt to play strange pranks, to throw off odd conceits, whims, and notions. For instance, consider Queen Victoria whose memory is the subject of three separate and distinct traditions at least, and may possibly give rise to others before time shall be dissolved in eternity. Her first tradition, as it were, begins when first she came to the throne, and this tradition is generally favourable to her throughout its course; the second begins about the time when the death of her husband caused her to withdraw herself from the public gaze, and endures till the retirement that she had sought for a while was brought to an end; but generally speaking this tradition is uncomplimentary to her; and the third extends from her reappearance on the stage of public affairs till her death in the year 1901 : but this tradition I venture to think a good deal too flattering to her. A somewhat similar cycle of crystallizations is now making touching her successor, Edward VII; but, as yet, the process spoken of has not produced more than two traditions, one of which applies to the years during which he was on the throne, the other having to do with his memory since his death. I think at this conjuncture to make a few brief observations as to both these matters.

The poet, seeking to determine the origin of fancy, sets it, sensibly enough, 'in the heart or in the head,' and a similar restriction or narrowing as to choice, and a like ascription as to beginnings, should, I suppose, serve our turn as well with regard to this matter of tradition, whose fount or birthplace apparently is, like the other, the hearts or heads of men. The alternative proffered by the poet is advisable, even necessary, since, speaking generally, there are two distinct sorts of traditions, namely, the sort which is popular by origin and nature, and so is of the heart, and that, on the other hand, which is the effect of applied study, of schools and scholars and their writings, and thus this latter kind of tradition is of the nature of the head. Generally speaking, too, the tendency of event as regards the sort of tradition first mentioned is that it yields in time to the second, to become absorbed by it, on the principle that the emotions of the heart are commonly less strong and penetrating, and less capable to endure, than those of the head.

Among several psychological causes of tradition in general is national pride. Indeed, national pride and self-esteem, mixed with some racial superstition, are commonly very important elements of it, and for this reason they must needs be taken into serious account. These qualities then are the yeast which cause tradition to swell in the making of it, to rise much above the level of the other ingredients before this strong addition to them was made. We see this truth well illustrated in the case of Queen Victoria, who, allowing that she was a woman of a very considerable talent, and knew the business of a sovereign extremely well, yet most certainly was not the great figure which the subjects in general have come to believe that she was in life, no matter what Strachey, and others who have written in the same sense touching the queen, and the part she played in public affairs, may affirm to the contrary.   Farther, it is being illustrated at the present time, that is through the channel of some who wish the world in general to believe that, though he was not so great a figure as Victoria, yet the late King Edward was in some sort a sufficient successor to her, though nothing can be plainer, nothing nearer truth, than that his whole performance as a sovereign was negligible, and, farther, that his parts, no matter what their particular merits might be, little justify the drawing this odd comparison.   It should seem, then, on a review of both these cases, that the ordinary Englishman's strong, though perhaps natural, esteem for himself and his race, for his country, its institutions and representative figures, has led him here to force tradition beyond the bounds which, strictly speaking, are proper to it, and thus has he made of it, in these two instances at least, a species of exaggeration in room of a reasonable statement of as reasonable truth.

I suppose that were one asked to produce parallels and resemblances of nature in respect of the late King Edward and some of his

predecessors on the English throne, he would
immediately alight on the eighth King Henry
and George IV. But should this happen to
any one, and the comparison glanced at seem
to him just, he would do well not to draw it
in either case too close or too strict, or yet to
follow it too far; since though some appearances may unite to flatter the notion, yet surely
much and deep deception lurks beneath them.
For instance, though King Edward by no means
lacked ability, nor yet astuteness, and showed
on occasions much soundness of judgment with
regard to public affairs, nevertheless he had not
the genius for politics which Henry of England
most certainly had, no matter how rash and
artless the methods which he used in pursuit
of his political ends might be at times; nor,
though King Edward loved music and had considerable knowledge and understanding of the
science of it, had he the aesthetic sensibility,
and love of art, of George IV, assuming that
that which is now said in this way in behalf
of this prince is truth, and not partisan pleading, or stuff such as 'whitewashers' use in the
course of their operations. It is plain, therefore, that though a general resemblance of
things to one another, or that of a person or
persons to other natures in history, is ground

enough for some guarded comparison, yet in neither case must the resemblances be pushed too far; much less must the deductions drawn from them resemble in spirit the famous laws of Medes and Persians.

Like a deal of human nature, the late King Edward was a compound of different qualities, some good, some indifferent, and yet a few that answer to neither of these sorts; and if I prefer here to speak first, though in the briefest manner, of his defects, it is because they were the principal cause of his failure to profit by the others, in fine to render his brief tenure of the sovereignty distinguished.

He was always pleasure-loving, and therefore averse from study and application. He had, I think, conversed at times with his own shadow, had he not been a king and therefore ever able to command company. He practised no sort of private retirement, and to his nature study and solitariness were disagreeable. Badinage, jesting, anecdote, rumour, report, company-fireworks, and broad and familiar story—these distractions were to his mind as meat is, in general, to the body. His temper, otherwise, was careless and indolent, and his range of interests much restricted by his tastes, which gave rise to habits that interfered with the exercise of his intellect; but this last, though by no means inconsiderable, yet was hardly of the first quality. He thought that the English monarchy, and the monarchial cause and principle generally in Europe, were in a languishing state; but whether he indulged this opinion in order to soften to himself and excuse to others his inactivity touching the political rights of the English Crown, or whether, on the other hand, he believed it sincerely, is in some sort immaterial, since the effects were the same, both with regard to himself and the throne. He had a good knowledge of men, could probe motives, search situations, and forecast the results of ordinary conjunctures as well as any one about him, if not better than most; but then his own long neglect of study in his youth, conjoined with his own very slender powers of application to business when he was grown up, stood ever in the way of his benefiting, as he might have benefited, by virtue of such talent as he had, the Crown and realm of England.

He had much good-nature;[1] and a power of memory in respect to the faces of some of his subjects that was near extraordinary. I

[1] He once said with a smile to a kinsman of mine: 'Tell him' (meaning the present writer) 'that if he and I had lived in former times I would have had his head.'

mention this seemingly trivial feature of his character, because the faculty itself appears to be popular nowadays, and farther, because it appears to be an object of study with princes themselves, who may possibly see in it a substitute of sorts for lost prerogative. Of that sort of kindliness in princes which moves them on occasions — as one reads in the press — to help lame dogs over stiles, or old women with their baskets, he had little or nothing, I think: on the other hand, his good-nature, his tolerance, and dislike of strife and contention, ever inclined him much to fair dealing and peaceful measures. Generally, too, he was considerate of others, and courteous to all. Indeed, he was best pleased, and, I think, best employed, when he was busy reconciling animosities, fomenting alliances, softening estrangements, smoothing ruffled countenances and counselling forbearance, over a well-laden table; but then to ascribe to these convivial gatherings, and the part he took in them, a significance of state entirely out of proportion, as well to the occasions of them as to their effects in politics, is plainly absurd, though this, too, has been done. He was popular with his ministers, because he was ever forward to practise that which they wished him to do, which rendered

him, in their eyes, a good monarch, according
to the constitution as they saw it and the king
as they construed him; but what the king himself may have thought within himself, touching the wisdom of some of these advices and
the authors of them, is of course a different
matter—a secret whose opening is postponed
till the rest shall be made known.

To be (as indeed befits) candid touching King
Edward, his principal misfortune in life—apart
entirely from his strong disinclination to study,
and to retirement for purposes of study—was
that he had so little comprehension of the fact
that the Crown was yet in some sort a reality
of importance, despite the many signs and
symbols of decay that now were settled thick
about it. If Louis XIV was apt to jest, as
Bolingbroke relates of him, touching the little
education he had, the Prince of Wales was often
heard to speak flippantly of the institution of
monarchy, and, farther, of his own elevation to
the throne as an event not very like to come to
pass, nor, in any case, particularly desired by
him. Thus, when he came to enter English
monarchy—in short, to represent it in his own
person—he was spiritually far from being all of
a piece with it. Till the year of his succession
he had doubted it pretty consistently—made

light of it, even ridiculed it at times, in room of giving to it his respect and his serious study; and though the probability, nay the reasonable certainty, is that towards the close of his life and reign his Crown and the 'business' of it became as great with him as ever his idle pleasures had been so formerly, yet now it was too late: Death, with the Successor behind him, was already knocking at the door of the Seventh Edward.

Speaking of Louis XIV, Lord Bolingbroke says in the letter on the study of history from which I have quoted already, that 'if he was not the greatest king, he was the best actor of majesty at least that ever filled a throne'; but Edward VII deserves not to be reckoned above any of those 'little actors' of majesty, 'whose subject is too slight to descend to posterity in any other manner' than by their appearance in the list of the kings and queens of the countries whose thrones they came to fill for a while.

GLADSTONE

CHAPTER II

GLADSTONE

EVERY man is susceptible to be divided into
a number of separate parts, that is natures,
and every woman perhaps into a multitude
of these spiritual objects. But on the present
occasion I propose to divide Gladstone into
three only, one of which is ecclesiastic, another
rhetorician, and the third politician; for, to
my mind, he was ever too much a party-man
to be, by temper and breeding, a statesman, in
the 'classic' sense of the word at least.

It happens often in this life that nature
seems to design a man to a particular end, a
particular avocation, profession, or calling; but
is crossed in this design by the man himself,
who is drawn by interest or ambition, or it may
be by circumstance alone, into some other way
of life, and therefore disappoints in some sort
nature's intention, as well as his own genius.
I think Gladstone was born into this order of
men; but then one day something stepped in
'twixt the intention of his birth and himself,

and he became a politician in room of a cleric. A turn of the hand of chance is sometimes sufficient to change the whole course of destiny, even as a feather cast into a scale may disturb at once the true balance of it.

If, as I suppose, Gladstone was born for a parson, he had risen for sure from that situation upwards, through a succession of lesser ecclesiastical honours, even to an archbishopric, in which capacity, and the Church of England as by law established, I think he had excelled, since his whole mind, nature, and outlook on life were so entirely formed to ecclesiastical ends, and since he had so very considerable a genius, and powerful a personality, besides. He had so strict Anglican views, and so much particularism was mixed with them, besides a deal of very odd history and yet stranger theology, that I cannot imagine him situated outside the bounds—if indeed such restrictions it possesses at all — of the Anglican Church. Were it otherwise, I could well imagine him a cardinal of very great eminence, a morally improved Wolsey or a more 'liberal' Anselm: his mind, too, had some points of contact with Borromeo, though I doubt much if he had any of the saint's diplomatic ability. In any event, his whole attitude towards politics was ever sacerdotal, or rather druidical, and in all his public speeches and formal addresses, the natural bent of his nature appears very plainly.

Still, it was not to his Church that Gladstone turned, or was turned, when he was young, but to politics, which he entered in much the same spirit apparently as marked in general the youth of breeding of a bygone age, when they entered on the round of visits to European countries which fashion prescribed, and their sires mapped out, for them. He rose with fair rapidity, and with promise and performance enough to give colour to a notion that was had of him by some at that time, namely, that the name of Gladstone might yet appear to advantage in the annals of English party politics. But this is no place for a long, or even a brief, detail of my subject's political career, which has been related already with an industry, and set forth with a skill and a fullness, such as the occasion of this career demands most certainly of any one who may aspire to describe it.

His public speech was sonorous, and flowed like the waters of a noble river. He had a wonderful gift of parenthetical remark, and a power of carrying on the sense, or rather

senses—developing and even adding to them
on the road—of one long passage into another,
if not into a series of them, that moved one
to admiration as often as he heard him. He
used little imagery, and employed not much
wit, in which, I think, he was deficient; and as
small a sense of humour as I have seen in any
man whose gift of eloquence is admitted generally, marked him most evidently. He had,
too, a vast command of platitude, which en-
abled him to sway audiences as completely
as the poet who has, in a like measure, the
same gift, and exerts it in his writings, sways
the minds of his critics and his readers. His
private speech was harangue, rather than conversation; and on every word of it his family
and dependants, his henchmen, intimates, and
immediate followers generally, were used to
hang, as though it were suspended miracle.
However, I do not think that the adulation
which he received in this way, though continuous, and laid on thick enough to spoil any
man, yet affected him injuriously, though it
certainly had the effect of encouraging him to
prolonged discourse, to call the tune of conversation more often than was creditable to
him, or convenient to some of his listeners at
least. He had too fine a nature, and, since he

was a strictly religious man, was too well
grounded in humility to be seduced by flattery, which is perhaps the basest of the several
means by which the lesser seek to curry favour
with the greater natures of this world, or discover their fear of them, or temper their awe
of them.

I remember that on one occasion I defended
ri aghaidh, to his face, as we say in Gaelic,
the memory of our King James III—I mean
him that was father to James IV, not the later
Stewart prince so styled by English Jacobites—
who has been traduced by our historians,
though by what authority (save their own)
and on what grounds, save those collected by
his enemies, does not appear; who follow one
another in this matter as indeed they do generally, that is to say, like geese that walk in
single file. He listened to my defence in
silence; and, when it was done, said no more
than that he understood that James was ruled
by favourites. He opened then some other
topic, on which he proceeded to harangue the
company at immense length, and, I thought,
to very little purpose. The theme had not
interested him; and, besides, of it he had
no more knowledge than can be collected by
any one from our historical textbooks; and,

farther, I think that in it he suspected, so far
as I was concerned, an anti-Reformation cabal—
a sort of 'popish plot,' possibly to blow up
the memory of Buchanan, who was probably
father to all the lies glanced at, as well as
the undoubted progenitor of many touching
our Queen Mary, which passed current in
those days (and for many years thereafter)
as readily as the others do in these. He ever
suspected, and was always much on his guard
against, oblique engagements of this nature, a
thing which the part he played touching the
matter of the validity of Anglican Church
Orders proves sufficiently, I think.

The sort of rhetoric he employed on public
occasions was well fitted to please Scottish
audiences, which love eloquence and a com-
bative address, in fine, a 'fighting-man,' as
some old scribe, a Greek or a Roman—I
forget which of them for the moment—observed
of the Celts many centuries ago. Whether
it was art, necessity, or natural propensity of
mind that led him to mix with his speeches,
not religion, but an air of intense righteousness, I am not very sure; but since the quality
of man himself is very mixed, I suppose that
either of the usages mentioned, and doubtless
all of them at times, came to him naturally

enough. In any event, he was ever immensely popular in Scotland. A pretty woman that looks much into her mirror does so presumably because she is pleased with the reflection she finds there. The Scottish nation was used for a long time to look into the mirror of Gladstone; and, seeing itself in some sort reflected there, it was pleased with both, very naturally. Sometimes he recollected that though himself was bred an Englishman, yet his parentage was Scottish; and as often as he recalled to mind the fact I mention, or was reminded of it by others, he spoke of it with pride, with emphasis, and a solemnity which I for one found somewhat diverting, considering how little he really knew of the country of his ancestors, its true history, and native civilization and culture. To say truth, his interest in it was almost entirely party, and, when and where it was not so, purely senti-mental, which means, I suppose, that his feelings about it were neither particularly well informed, nor yet very sure or deep. I told him once an amusing anecdote which an old Aberdeen-shire laird, a great Jacobite, had told me touching Queen Victoria and her particular body - servant, John Brown. The latter, it appears, was somewhat sceptical regarding the

sincerity of his royal mistress's professions of
esteem for Scotland, and things Scottish generally; or it may be that he presumed to doubt if
Her Majesty had any real ground for it in a
true knowledge of either, and this doubt of one
kind or the other he once had the front to
let out to her, 'twixt his hand and his side,
to use a native idiom; when he was soundly
rated by the queen for his pains, and even
banished her immediate service for a while.
Gladstone laughed at the anecdote; but I saw
from his countenance, and the air generally
with which he had received it, that he had
no thought whatever to apply to himself the
lesson of it. My arrow had flown harmlessly
above the great man's head.

What a man designs is not necessarily that
which comes to pass with him; and even
though he achieve that which he has set before
him, yet often will the event differ in part,
and notably, from his first anticipations and
intentions; and possibly from his hopes, in
as plain a manner; so that his last fortune
may well come to bear very little resemblance
to his first notions.   This observation is made,
not to introduce platitude to the reader, but
to remind him of Oliver Cromwell and W. E.
Gladstone; the first of whom designed a great

confederacy of Protestant states in the West, and completely failed in it, but gave nevertheless to Puritanism in England its death-blow as a ruling power; and the second of whom aimed to establish in the same country a sort of Whiggish *Civitas Dei*, ruled by a caucus compounded of Liberal free-thinkers of good repute and social standing and Nonconformist conscience, headed and presided over by himself; but who came to die, after a long life, devoted mainly to 'business,' as he understood and practised it, without doing more towards it than laying this design, as well as the seeds of the disruption of his own party. Which has happened since.

Three men there are that I consider as in some sort spiritual complements to one another in English history; and the three men I intend are Cromwell, Gladstone, and General Booth, in each of whom I discern elements of greatness, though none of them, I think, was more than relatively, and therefore not positively, great.

The natures of Gladstone and General Booth had a deal in common; and though these two spirits approximated to one another in this way more than either did so to Cromwell, or Cromwell to them, yet I make bold to think that the ascription I have made is just enough,

and the triumvirate I have set up reasonable
enough. The soldier drew his sword, and
with it attacked prerogative and privilege;
but always (even in compassing his king's
death) from what he took to be a religious
motive, from the highest principles, and
the strictest notions of human conduct that
can be. At least so he professed, and his
followers believed. Gladstone laboured to
introduce 'righteousness' into the English
political world, and, from thence, into European public affairs generally; and if this 'righteousness' to which he sought to persuade
mankind was in a manner peculiar to himself,
and little like to be approved by the world
in general (which indeed fell out), yet the
fact of his so apposite apostleship remains:
so that, be it agreeable or be it the reverse
to us, his light is there, and burns for all to
see. Booth, neither a soldier nor yet a politician to trade, nevertheless partook in some
sort of both these types, giving to the society
which he formed a distinctively military frame-
work, and cast of countenance, and a title
to it, besides, which since it denotes, in part
at least, 'uplift,' is of the order, in the cate-
gories, of civil politics, which, like the older
and superior kind, must ever aim at social

'betterment,' or perish in the esteem of men.
Time may disband the army that he raised,
bad generalship lead it to disaster, or ill discipline within the ranks dissipate it; but these
are contingencies of fortune that appear as
such only to the eye of this age; but, coming
to pass in some shape or other, may yet form
a part of the religious experience of the next;
though in the meanwhile the host of marching
filles du régiment in poke-bonnets, and colpor-
teurs in military array, with bands and banners
at their head, endures, and, I suppose, continues
to draw numerous recruits to it.

It was a principle of gain, of interest, that
united for a while Caesar, Pompey, and Crassus,
and kept, for the same while, the first triumvirate in being; but then the first, and
perhaps the last, triumvirate of English history
is formed, and acts therein, on a very different
bottom. There is Caesar, who is Cromwell;
Pompey, who is Gladstone, and Crassus, who
is Booth, rich in ideas, if not wealthy, even as
the Roman plutocrat was so; but the tie which
unites these English three, and keeps them
together in the mind of history, is, not gain,
but righteousness, that surprising product of
the English nature turned religious, which is,
I suppose, to be dated from Reformation times,

but strong traces of which occur much earlier in history, as every discerning student of the national story of the people I name will allow very freely, I doubt not. Some might say, and should they say it I think they would have warrant enough, that mixed with the purer and nobler elements of this 'righteousness' is a good deal of intolerance, of hypocrisy, of narrow-mindedness, of pride, of ill odour, of stale presumption, of illiberality of opinion, of sanctimoniousness, of self-flattery and self-congratulation: all which the English, as a whole, seem as prone to practise as they are prone to bread sauce and boiled potatoes in their kitchen, to halting speakers in their rostrums, dull performers in their pulpit, and as bad in their music. But these and other punctilios of a kind suggested by the present theme, I must not allow to delay or divert me: I propose, then, to conclude this head with a few final observations.

There are minds which, looking not so much into their own, but others', find therein many kinds of blemishes, and imperfections of a more serious nature; at which they are apt to marvel, and of which they are used to complain, according as their different humours move them, forgetting apparently that their

own minds and natures are formed precisely
to these, and nowise differ from them essentially. Gladstone has been much criticized
by biographers, by memoir-writers and party-
scribes in general, who plod through his life like
a countryman through a heavy field, and seem
surprised at the end, and not a little shocked,
to find there what any man of sense could have
told them before, that, soon or late, they must
surely find, namely, that through Gladstone's
public life, as through those of others of his
kind, and all such lives in general, if not indeed
all through life considered as a whole, a thread
of occasional inconsistency of speech and conduct plainly runs.   They who are fond to make
mountains of mole - hills, and mighty rivers
of insignificant streams, will doubtless observe
a similar geography, when they come to man,
and propose to themselves a reasoned detail
of his collective nature, his acts, and his
achievements, his passions, follies, absurdities,
and whimsicalities; but to the rest of us doubtless this meticulous analysis, this too free,
too prodigal, and too continuous use of the
searchlight will seem unnecessary and a tedious
business.   To say truth, Gladstone's political
career and performance, considered indepen-
dently of his immediate personality, are, to

the present writer at least, if not to the youth
of the age we live in, from whom, however,
mutterings to the same effect have been heard
before now, singularly bare and superlatively
uninteresting, my own belief being, by consequence, that it matters nothing nowadays what
thread of inconsistency runs through Gladstone's life, as it runs through all others, seeing
that the springs of the charge against him are no
longer of moment to the living world. It is
possible that Freud, or some other professor
of legerdemain, might, by a single observation
of the axe wherewith Gladstone was used to
fell trees, discover to us the secret springs of
all the inconsistencies laid at the latter's door;
but though he, or any one else like to him,
should work this wonder for us, how would
it benefit us, or enlarge experience; since all
flesh is inconsistent, and human nature un-
changeable essentially?

As I think on Gladstone, and ponder his
career, I imagine to myself the figure of an
eagle. The eagle stands on a pinnacle of a
rock in a mountain - side, in a country full of
grandeur, where all is solitude and remoteness;
canopied with cloud, and little lighted, save
here and there, far below the great bird's
eyrie, by gleam of loch or glint of river. It

may be that even to this eagle that stands,
preparing his flight towards the mists of dawn,
something yet is wanting—that his plumage
is less lustrous, his markings less strong,
his whole power of being as a son of the
heavens less plain to the eye than these things
are plain in others of his kind.   But no matter:
this one also is of the breed of the lords of
the air, and the princes of their species; winged
familiars of the storm and the cataclysms of
nature, born lookers-in-the-face of sun and
lightning.

JOHN REDMOND

CHAPTER III

JOHN REDMOND

I FIRST met the late John Redmond in Ireland, on the occasion of Parnell's last political campaign. I was introduced to him, and his brother, Willie, by the Irish leader. John impressed me at once very favourably; but Willie I thought much less a figure than the other.

The latter I found very good company, full of animal spirits, but too effervescent by half to inspire much confidence as to his parts. He was boyish beyond his years: the jest and that sort of easy badinage, witty to some extent, and good-humoured enough, in which I think the Irish excel, and most certainly indulge more than do most peoples, were too often on his lips, I judged, to conceal any deeper nature than he showed. I thought him, too, not over-well grounded in national principle. In fine, the opinion I formed of him at the time was that his nature resembled a cork that floats on the breast of waters that run rapidly, and that is carried, this way and that, by the stream, bobbing, and riding the wavelets in jaunty fashion, never long submerged, but often out of sight, sucked under water, as it is hurried along. He was hurried, before his end came, into society and measures which consorted but ill with some of the sentiments I heard him express on the occasion I refer to, and that he was fond to give a loose to, many a time, afterwards. But I believe that had he got better instruction than he received apparently, and had his nature been less volatile than it was, he would have avoided one and eschewed the other. However, peace to his soul! He was a most likeable man.

It was very different with his brother, John: at least, I found it so. I found immediately that his nature 'filled the eye,' to employ a Gaelic and a very expressive idiom. His speech and carriage were grave—suggesting that large reservations of intellectual power lay in him— and of almost senatorial dignity already, though he was but a very young man when I came to know him first. Parnell leaned on him much: he was his favourite lieutenant, I think; and, for my part, I thought the choice well made; for of all those that were about the Irish leader at the time, it seemed to me that John Redmond was much the most promising figure, by far the most fit to don the mantle of leadership when Parnell himself should cease to wear it.

It is surely a question that deserves, and demands of us, some thought, whether to be born into this world before one's time or after it, as it were, is the greater inconvenience, the greater disability, as regards the person that undergoes this experience. To be born in advance of one's time, as it were, is misfortune; but then to me it seems no less misfortune to be born into the past, again 'as it were.' For he whose whole mind and nature are bent to the future, and thus can have but little or no root at all in the present (which surely is his true province of being in both senses of the word), must be greatly incommoded, vastly hampered, by reason of this, his fate, since on most of the ordinary, and certainly on all the extraordinary, occasions of life, he will be at loggerheads with his times and contemporaries. On the other hand, if it happen to a man that he is born so as to live in the past, instead of the present, ten to one but that man will be inconvenienced in like manner, and, I suppose, in the same degree, as the other; since he will find that the most of his contemporaries are not only indifferent to the past, but ignorant of

it, and very impatient of it as well. On the
whole matter, then, it should seem that he
whose birthday, as it were, is betwixt the two
extremes in time of past and future; who sits
at neither of these two poles, but midway
between them, that is, in the present, is ever
better situated as regards the chances and the
prizes of this life than the others provided
that he has knowledge and understanding of
the past, and talent and discernment enough
to apply this knowledge (together with that
which he has collected from the present, and
digested) to the future—a mystery no doubt
to all of us; but yet a mystery that will yield
some at least of its secrets to him that has
access to the keys of human experience, and
is skilled, too, in the use of them.   Thus, the
summum bonum of the worldly philosophy is, not
where Nietzsche sought to set, and others of
this age think, it, that is, in the 'power-to-
will,' so as to bind men, and causes, and even
whole societies; but in this very knowledge
I speak of—in fine, in a man's capacity so to
mix ideals with realities as to effect, in respect
of the two, a balance or proportion as near
perfect as can be.   He then who has the
'keys' has surely something better than all
the spells and 'sciences,' philosophers' stones

and liquors of life that ever were, or pretended
to be.

But to resume: John Redmond's spiritual
home lay in the past; and here, too, were
lodged the first causes of all his hopes, his
aims and ambitions. However, it was not
in the remote past either of his country, or
the West generally, that the spiritual roots of
Redmond, a politician, were firmly planted;
but in O'Connell, who died in 1847, and therefore in the same century in which John himself
was born. He had no great knowledge of the
past history of his country; just that smatter-
ing of it only which a leading man of affairs
in Ireland (such as he was) was apt to find useful on a public platform in those days—in order
to trim a peroration to a speech, to illustrate
minor points of political debate, or to enlarge
current topics of the same nature; though I
doubt not that if Irish scholarship had been
more advanced than it was at the period of
which I now speak, John had addressed himself
to it with all imaginable zeal and application;
for he was interested in archaeological matters,
and gave, too, some thought and time to
speculation touching the originals of his country,
slender though these informations then were,
relatively to what is known about them to-day.

There was something Romanesque about
O'Connell, and therefore there was something
Romanesque about Redmond also. The resemblance I speak of was not, I think, entirely
accidental by nature; nor is it, I think, a mere
sally of imagination on my part, though such,
I allow, it might well be judged but for —
among other proofs to the contrary—Irish
Romanesque, a very beautiful style of architecture that the Irish practised early, and a
few examples of which remain to adorn the
country of its birth. This singularly agreeable
consequence of the union of two separate and
distinct styles of architecture (the native or
Celtic and the Roman) was a consequence, I
suppose, of 'classic' influences, which were
early both rife and powerful in Ireland, and discovered themselves there in more ways than
it would be possible to mention in this place.
And that which (no matter what its origin)
comes to be bred in the bone of the aesthetic
sense and sensibility of a people, and thus is
of its genius as regards the practice of the arts
generally, and is transmitted by it from generation to generation, from age to age; this
quality, I say, is very apt to appear in the flesh
also, that is, in particular individuals, in social
manners and customs, and ways of life generally.

Certainly O'Connell was a good deal shaped on a 'classic' model, which is plain from his different writings and speeches; and this bent or bias to 'classicism' that was in him, Redmond, consciously or unconsciously, contracted or assumed, perhaps from long study of these same models; but, in any event, from O'Connell most certainly.

He had a fine gift of oratory. His public speech at its best was grave, ordered, dignified—solid and imposing, as are the best examples of the Roman architecture; and here I beg leave to propose to myself a short digression: I do not believe that the pretended everlasting union of the two principles of art and utility, of which so much is spoken and written with easy confidence these days, is truth. In short, I think the two qualities named absolutely distinct, as far from one another in aesthetic experience as the mutual repulsion of contraries can set them; though I allow freely enough that where art is employed in order to improve, or at all events to de-vulgarize, the appearance of objects that are the effect of the utilitarian principle or motive, the saying that the end justifies the means may here receive some justification at least. But I cannot allow more. In fine, I think that the genius of

Roman architecture was but the Greek genius
in respect of the same thing, the first being
differentiated from the second, but in so far
only as the Greek genius and the Roman genius
differed from one another. Therefore, when
I say that Redmond was used to make speeches
comparable to those of Romans, and, farther,
that these speeches were solid and dignified
as Roman public buildings, it is the aesthetic
and spiritual qualities of Redmond's orations
that I have in mind in venturing this comparison, and not the utilitarian cause or principle
of the objects to which I have likened them.

I remember that when it was cried in the
lobbies that Redmond was 'up' to speak, the
chamber itself was used to fill rapidly; for
though few Englishmen appear to have much
gift of oratory, or understanding of the principles of it either, still they have two great
merits in this regard, namely, they will flock
to hear a good speaker (no matter what his
race or theme may be), and, secondly, very
commonly, they are extremely impatient of
their own countrymen who perform lamely in
this way, who, solid enough in other ways
perhaps, yet speak with all the little arts of
the public bore. He was as much sought and
admired in Ireland, too, by persons who had

an ear for oratory, as he was so honoured in
England. He came but rarely to Scotland;
but on those few occasions on which he spoke
in public among us the applause that greeted
him at the time, and commended his talent
afterwards in the press, was as spontaneous, as
generous and sincere, as any that he experienced
elsewhere.

But whether his gift of public speech was
accompanied with other talent as considerable
as this, he never showed, though to some he
gave good cause to believe that he would shine
as much in the council chamber as he did on
the platform, or in the House of Commons,
provided that the opportunity which he sought
came to him. Reserved natures are hard to
plumb, and potential or imputed gifts but so
many subjects of vain speculation. A man may
excite generally great expectations as to his
talent, and as to his powers of public performance; but if, though he should have the
means, no fit occasion or just opportunity of
exerting them should come his way, the expectations formed of this man must remain but
empty shadows. But one such occasion only
came to Redmond, which occurred during the
latter part of the reign of Edward VII, when
a convention was held by the administration

of the day in order to discover ways and means to settle, on what were styled 'constitutional lines,' the Irish problem. Redmond also was called to this convention, and to it he went; but he told me afterwards that what he found at it was an atmosphere little congenial to what he and his party thought and had long designed with respect to the matter which was then on the carpet. In any event, the convention broke down, and Redmond's grand opportunity to show what gift of statesmanship he might have, passed, and perished, with it.

The strategy used by the Irish parliamentary party at Westminster can be set forth in a very few words. It was this — a united front in the House of Commons, and heavy simultaneous agitation at home, in Ireland. Such was the policy of O'Connell, and, when the 'Tribune' died, of Butt, and, next, of Parnell. Redmond also was a votary to it, and carried it on with zeal, but with far too great faith in its efficacy, after he was elected to the leadership of the reunited party in the year 1900. He had good qualities of leadership, tact, 'presence,' address, acumen, courage, and a high sense of discipline and its virtues. He showed firmness of rule when, and where, firmness was needed. He knew some men very well; in the event the pity for him and his memory was, that he did not learn to know some others as perfectly.

The figure of the cloud on the horizon which at first is no bigger than a man's hand is, for all ages, peoples, persons, and occasions, a perpetual warning. Strange that so many to whom this sign appears neglect it! In their private affairs, different men and women by the thousand neglect it daily; but perhaps these are to be excused to some extent. But when, as often happens, whole nations and societies receive but give no heed to this warning, take no alarm whatever from it, this surely is lamentable—conduct like to excuse the severest censures ever passed on the human race. The warning came, in the appointed shape, to John Redmond, and he, too, though the head of a party, a man of talent, and experienced in the ways of the world, and to some extent at least a student (and a knowing one, too) of human nature, neglected it. It was not, however, that he did not see it; for he and his whole party saw it plain enough; and, besides, it was pointed out to him by others, many a time and oft; but that, seeing, yet he disbelieved, and, disbelieving, turned his back to it. His fault therefore was twofold; and agreeably to the measure of it was his punishment.

I have said already that Redmond was tied and bound by the plan of O'Connell's strategy. There was to be, as himself expressed it often, a 'fight on the floor of the House' and agitation at home, till the end which he and his party sought should be gained; and in the meanwhile political Ireland was to be kept lively in the same interest, by means of agitation designed to help the gaining elsewhere this particular end. The plan was simple, and, obviously, not without merit; but that at the same time it had its own share of drawbacks and dis-advantages—this, on the other hand, is, I think, no less plain.

I have heard it said formerly that the attrac-tions of London life were apt to work an ill effect on the discipline and morale generally, and so on the efficiency, of the Irish party; but for my part I think that the principal objection to O'Connell's plan lay in the fact that, as time went on, it tended to convention-alize and stereotype political endeavour, both on 'the floor of the House' and in Ireland itself. In a word, the party and its leaders became engrossed with the 'machine,' and neglectful of circumstance and opportunities in

proportion as they became engrossed with it.
Policies may appear, and flourish for a while;
but after a time they begin to fade, and pre-
sently, like the others, droop and die; and this
happened to the Irish parliamentarians.

As to Redmond in particular, I think that as
his leadership grew in years a sort of mental
blindness afflicted him. There was much writing on the wall about the time I have in mind;
but to these signs of impending pregnant
change in Ireland he closed his eyes. At
times it appeared to me that he would rather
hazard the cause than scrap the machine.
Strong natures under the influence of what
they think provocative measures are very apt
to make wrong judgments as to persons and
things; to allow pride, passion, and prejudice
to set aside the dictates of prudence, and the
little spites and rubs of life to entice them
into ways and conduct that are all unworthy
of them, and injurious, too, very often to the
cause they support.

The party of Sinn Fein declared for the
revival of the Irish language. I once questioned
Redmond as to this matter, and the reply I
got from him was, that as there were nations
that had no proper languages of their own,
but yet were independent, and respected by

their neighbours, as well as by the generality of men, therefore he saw no good reason why his own should labour the cause of the revival of their ancient but decaying speech. For answer, I told him that he had missed the point. 'Think you,' said I, 'that the Swiss or the people of the United States would suffer the national tongue to die, supposing that one or other of them had such a thing to revive? You know very well,' I said, 'that it would not be running but leaping with these nations, hastening to the rescue of the threatened tongue. Though the Irish language had no merit, whereas much it has, still, it would be worth the reviving; for it is Irish, which English is not nor can be ever.' He appeared to weigh and ponder the matter for a while; but I could see well that the example of O'Connell, who, though an Irish speaker, yet declared for English language for his countrymen, and his own jealousy of the Sinn Fein party, together with the strong dislike that he had of some of its leaders, would in the event conspire to make him turn away his face from the rising sun, and set it steadfastly towards the airt of death and shadows and departing glories—the West. And this, too, happened.

As the party of Sinn Fein began to rise to

power in Ireland, and that of the 'constitution-
alists' to descend in the scales of the national
interest, the irritation of which I have spoken
previously increased in him; and jealousy,
alarms as to the future, and disappointments
at this (to him) disappointing course of events
joined themselves together, so as to produce in
him a hardening of his first resolution, and,
subsequently, an obliquity of judgment that
seemed to me at least almost fanatical in its
intensity.   A degree of spite and hatred of
those who opposed his plans, and disputed
publicly as well his authority as the wisdom
of his policy, now appeared in all his public
speeches, and gave occasion of ridicule to many
in Ireland and out of it.   At this time he seemed
like a man who surrenders long-cherished
hopes with near every breath of his body that
he takes: often he withdrew himself to the
solitude of his private room at the House of
Commons, moodish, visibly despondent, ill-
humoured, and little inclined (for so I have
heard) to afford access and communion even
to such of his followers at Westminster as he
liked most, and trusted the more.

Still, late in the day though it now was,
and despite the fact that all appearances and
prospects in Ireland were now against him,

yet it was not yet too late for him to mend, to
recover himself, his party, and their common
fortunes, in such a fashion as would have re-
stored to them the power which they had
lost, re-endowed them with the prestige in
the country that had been taken from them by
the Sinn Fein party, if Redmond himself, even
at this so late hour, had but consented to lay
or drive out the spirit of old-time politics by
which he was possessed; to call in to his side
the dogs of pride and pique; to forget rubs, and
forgive crosses to his will, to make peace and
alliance with his Irish opponents. But then,
unfortunately for him, never could he persuade
himself, nor would he suffer others to persuade
him, to allow this course to come to pass.

One day that was there, I went down to the
House of Commons in search of him. I found
him in his private room, alone; and when I
entered he was standing hard by a window.
The day was wet and dismal, and the short
winter afternoon, charged with the murk and
gloom of the season, was falling fast to dusk;
and as he turned himself about to greet me a
vision of this now so lonely and so disappointed
man came to me. I saw him, gazing out through
yon window, at the glistening yard beyond, at
the falling rain and heavy skies, at the street

lamps, now lighting or already lit, at the hurrying crowds without the palace gates; but
seeing, at the same time, nothing of these
things—only the hand of fate, and his declining
fortunes, cursing them both, as man is apt to
do when the world that is about him and in
which all his hopes are centred totters, but
yet, of his own will and initiative, aught to
save himself and it he does not, nor yet
intends.

I urged him to what was plain at the time to
every man of sense, and was plain, I doubt not,
even to him, blind to his true interest though
he was become by reason of pride and pique,
and so long and great affection for the plans and
ways of other years, namely, that he should cast
off the chains that bound him, arise, and go
forth to lead his nation as he alone, I said,
could lead it, and might lead it yet, if he would
but make this sacrifice of the past, of all his
present jars and discontents. He refused me;
but always in the kindest manner. I think
he trusted to the magic of his voice to work
the wonder which that of his policy was powerless now to bring about in Ireland; but Ireland
herself soon pricked the gaudy bubble. The
trump of silver was sounded on high in Ireland
indeed; but, this time, few were the ears that

listened to it with wonder, or yet with more than a casual passing heed.

.   .   .   .   .   .

Far away, over the waves, and near the place where the sun sinks at eve into the ocean, is a group of isles, to which is commonly said in legend, if not more authentically, the 'Isles of Fortune'; and on one of this group (for so they say) is a cemetery, wherein is laid, never to be disturbed, all that remains of what appeared in former times by way of policy and plan, of forms of states and governments, of treaties and alliances, and much other similar witness to the wisdom, or folly, of man turned politician. Full in the shade of a spreading cedar tree which grows, with others of its kind, within the boundaries of this cemetery, is dug a grave, at whose head is set a stone, whereon appears, engraved, a single word: 'O'Connell'; whilst at the foot of it is yet another, but a lesser, stone, whereon these words are inscribed (though in somewhat smaller letters): 'John Redmond.' 'Twixt these two stones, and connecting them, is laid a third, on whose upper surface appears a writing, also engraved, whose purport is—according to the legend—that here lies buried all that remains of sundry

English Acts of Parliament—'Home-Rule Bills for Ireland' is how the story that records the fact describes them.

In the same cemetery, set here and there throughout it, and very numerous, are other headstones; but these are so decayed, so worn by time and spoiled by weather, that to read the writings that once were on them were now impossible to be done. Graves, too, are there which have no headstones to them; and some whose stonework is so fallen down, so overgrown with weed, encroaching thicket, and other spreading offspring of decay, that scarce a trace of them remains.

But yet another sort of graves is there (and of all the graves that throng yon distant place of burial, these, they say, are much the commonest); other graves are there whose state is neither good nor bad, nor new nor old, but, meanwhile, partakes of both conditions. These then are graves which, dug within the memory of living men, or beyond such memory by but a very little, seem new, when compared with the old; but old when compared with the new. Such inscriptions as are on them can still be plainly read; but dead and gone, scattered it may be to the ends of earth, or become indifferent to them, are they who caused and

once took care of them; and thus, on these
forgotten graves, the creeping moss begins
to invade the stone, and stains of weather and
of time appear, but warn in vain; the weeds
and grass grow rankly in their neighbourhood,
and on them fallen branch and leaf and twig
accumulate as time goes on; for no hand tends
them now, or heart remembers them.

HENRY ASQUITH

CHAPTER IV

HENRY ASQUITH

IF it be hard, as it is admittedly, to squeeze water from a stone, to extract humanism from a lawyer should seem wellnigh as difficult. There is apparently something in the nature of the legal profession that dries up those of such as engage with it; that narrows and cramps their minds and understandings, and so is apt to bring them to short pettifogging views of life and men, and human affairs in general. Still, it must be allowed that Henry Asquith had a deal of humanism; he was a scholar of parts, and took both pride and pleasure in the writings of the ancients, on which, indeed— as to the best of them—he modelled his whole style of public speaking, and, farther, to classic example he even in some sort conformed his whole social address. And yet to the end of his days he remained in appearance, in manner, and in his ways and habits of thought, very much the character in which he began his public career, that is to say, a lawyer. Apparently, the genius of his profession had too

firm a hold of him, and his own was too much
of a sort with it, to enable him to rid himself
of the disabilities glanced at, presuming that
he was conscious of and regretted them; and,
farther, endeavoured their removal, which,
however, does not appear.

The House of Commons in England swarms
with lawyers: they fly to it as moths to candles
or flies to carrion; and every little attorney
that comes to town imagines to himself a
woolsack in his suitcase, much as, in Napole-
onic times, each true foot-soldier of France
imagined to himself a *bâton* in his knapsack;
the consequence being that much bad and much
unnecessary law is hatched in the House of
Commons, and all roads to the drastic reduction
of the costs of legal processes (which are surely
scandalously high) are stopped most effectually.
In fine, if ever there was an interest, fully
'vested,' entrenched, and that has dug itself
in so deeply and securely that to root it out
were wellnigh impossible to be done, that
interest is English law, though, to be sure,
the principal reforming party in the place I
mention, which I suppose the Socialists take
to be themselves, is entirely blind to it, even
in respect of that eye which, by a stretch of
the imagination, may be allowed to be whole,

When he was yet a youth, and yet at school
in London, Asquith was distinguished above
his companions and classmates by his reticence,
by the care he took to frame with nicety his
speech, by his habit of withdrawing himself
occasionally from the society of his school-
fellows, and by devoting these intervals of
leisure to private thought and study. I
met him first at a Whig conversazione at
Edinburgh, a good few years before he came
to high office of any kind, though even then
he was thought by some of his party a most
promising man; but as yet not much considered
by the public in general, who had little attrac-
tion or liking to him, apparently. I was
introduced to him, as to the lady who was to
become his second wife, and conversed with
him for a while. We spoke, I remember,
of his party's prospects; and if what he said
on this occasion was much to the point, it
was rather good common sense than distinguished reflection.

I thought him not in place somehow at this
gathering, though he and the rest were all
Whigs. He was of a type of Englishman that
is ever English without a doubt throughout;
and of all political creeds, I judge Whiggery
to have been that which best consorted with

them.   There were Scots who were Whigs,
just as there were Scots who to-day are Socialists or Unionists, for no better reason than
that Whiggery came to the first, as Socialism
or Unionism appears to the second, that is to
say as forms of political diversion; but the
Scottic nature, I think, is too self-centred,
too prone to the things that are of itself, too
impatient of foreign example and innovation,
to form long and sincere attachments in respect
of the theories and the doctrines of other
peoples.   It will be remembered, I doubt not,
that even that part of our nation which declined
to Reformation principles was not long disposed to abide by the counsels of Geneva,
though Calvin came much nearer to the Scottish mind than ever any English or German
Protestant pundit did or could.   This matter
of the effect of religious theory and doctrine
on national natures needs fuller inquiry and
better illustration than it appears to have
received as yet at the hands of the learned.

It is always interesting, if not in some cases
very fruitful, to compare, to co-ordinate, particular natures with others of the same, or near
the same, type that have preceded the others
in a point of view of time.   There are not a
few Whigs of previous generations that suggest

more or less plausible, and more or less lively, parallels in respect of Asquith and themselves; such, for instance, as Halifax (author of the *Trimmer* study), Somers, and Carteret. Of these, perhaps the nearest in respect of the present subject is Somers, though points, as well of resemblance as positive contact, are to be discerned, I think, in respect of him and the other two also. Somers was an inveterate Whig, and, like Asquith, bred in the law. He, too, had a starched mind, a defect from which Asquith suffered also, though he had not the gross John Bullishness of the former, who once observed, on some occasion of a suggested peace with France, that for his part he had been bred in a hatred of the French, and did not think to let go of it now to please any man. Somers was ambitious and fond of office; and in this Asquith conformed to him; but then he had far more, and better, talent than the able but hard-faced placeman I name. Still, the fact that both men were lawyers, both Whigs, that both rose from small beginnings to honours and great appointments, that both won peerages for themselves, and that both had much the same texture of mind and share of the spirit of the Englishman, gives sanction, I think, to this brief likeness and

comparison. As to the other figures, I leave it
to the reader to collect from them, and their
respective public careers, such points of comparison and resemblance as the nature of the
present remarks may suggest to them.

Asquith passed through the outskirts of party
politics much as a knowing young pike makes
its way through the shallows towards the deep
waters of the loch it inhabits. I intend nothing
disrespectful to the memory of Asquith by
this figure of speech; but what I much intend
to convey is, that his political progress was,
though slow, yet ever steady, and full of
circumspection on his part. He had shrewd
notions as to his own interests in public life;
and talent, phlegm, and address enough to
push them with just so much persistence,
aplomb, and resolution as were necessary in
order to enable him—a 'new man' in the
party and without many friends in it at first—
to make himself known to it, and in some sort
indispensable to it.

To call a man, his actions, and his whole
career 'brilliant' is little temptation nowadays;
because the epithet is hackneyed, as much
blown upon by vogue and the extravagance of
writers as is that of 'great.' Near every other
writer, especially near every other novelist,

that appears in type nowadays, the critics
who review him think 'brilliant,' by which
they prove that they lack judgment, or have
no true standards by which to test merit, or
measure talent, in letters, or yet, wanting to
themselves both these requisites, have fallen
into this habit of florid indiscrimination
out of complaisance to the practice which
they ply among themselves. It is obvious,
however, that if to every other head brillian-
tine be applied, though the effect may be
decorative, yet hardly will it be impressive.
Epithets, surely, should be strictly proportioned to the subjects and occasions that
call them forth from the writer's store of
them; they should not be bandied about from
one lip to another like jests, lest, like jests
that are so indiscriminately used, and therefore
abused, they lose force and point, contour
and precision in course of the process; and,
finally, become like to them—mangled, soiled,
and wellnigh meaningless. For this reason,
but more particularly because I do not think
that it was in the power of Asquith's nature
to be brilliant, I refrain from applying to him
this popular epithet, and content myself instead
to describe him as a political plodder of exceptional industry and extraordinary powers;

for I think that if there was indeed in Asquith
a spark of genius somewhere, his reticence
and self-restraint, his excessive prudence and
caution, conjoined with the coldness of all
his parts and nature, conspired to hide it
from every judging eye, save of course his
Maker's.

I suppose that one and all of us are apt at
times to look into the magic mirror of history,
discerning therein, more or less plainly, ourselves, who, touched by the wand of this
imaginative proceeding, proceed to take shape
in the form of some one or other of the famous
figures we see to move and have their being
there. We may not, and no doubt such happens
not unseldom, choose with judgment; we may
not know ourselves yet, or the true natures and
achievements of those who strike our fancy,
leading us to compare ourselves to them, to
wish devoutly that we, too, might shine, dif-
fuse our light among men, even as did these
others, who, though long since dead and gone,
yet live in history. What day-dreams are
these, and what day-dreams we indulge!

Doubtless, Asquith also looked into the
mirror I speak of; and the choice he made was,
I think, Cromwell. To insist that on this
great figure of English history he sought to

model himself, even as the potter moulds
the clay in his hands, that is, so that it may
conform it to the pattern he has set before
him, would be absurd exaggeration, none of
my seeking, and opposed to my intention.
The probability which I claim is merely this,
namely, that, of all the figures of great Englishmen which the page of their story presents to
the race, this, I think, was the one that appealed
the most to Asquith, that excited his admiration
the most, that warmed his frigid nature, and
stirred his sluggish imagination the most; that,
ghost-like, haunted, as it were, his life the
most.

Our guardian angels are appointed to us
in order that they may take care of us, all
through our life: such never leave us till death
occurs; and the warnings and the counsel
they give us, these they are ever ready and
forward to proffer, no matter how deaf may
be the ear, and stubborn and irresponsive the
heart, to which these healthful whisperings
are addressed. But it is different with the
spirits which we of ourselves appoint to ourselves, or, all unconsciously, allow to have
direction over us. These spirits or familiars are
profane by origin and in nature; they are not
concerned with other than worldly ends, nor

seek, nor are called to our society by ourselves, but occasionally.

I think that one of these occasions occurred when Asquith joined himself to Rosebery, and the latter's little group of 'Liberal Imperialists.' I think, too, that another occurred when Asquith went to war so far at least as to become Minister for it at home. Surely, too, if, as was commonly said at one time, and is still repeated on occasions, *am Fear ud thall* (the One that is yonder) was the first Whig, Cromwell was the first 'Liberal Imperialist.'

For 'Liberal Imperialism,' and the institution of war, were both opposed to Asquith's nature, to his breeding, and to what he believed in his heart and conceived in his mind touching politics in general; and for these reasons my notion is that he embraced the one and, in the manner and to the extent glanced at, dabbled in the other, because the hero I have ascribed to him, namely Cromwell, strove to extend the English sway both in these isles and abroad, and therefore he also, though the head of a commonwealth or republic, yet was in some sort an imperialist; besides, every one knows that Cromwell was a famous commander —one of the best generals of cavalry that have ever lived, I have heard it said by critics of

military affairs whose judgment is worthy of
much respect. It often happens in life that
our natures are acted on, and our conduct
governed, by forces without us, but of which
we are unconscious, or at best but semi-
conscious—forces that often seek to drag us
(and what is more, sometimes succeed in doing
so) from our settled convictions: it may be
from our most stubborn prejudices; and, having
so far gained on us, leave us not till they have
set our feet on roads that are foreign to us, in
the sense that, were we left unmolested and
unconstrained by these forces, never should we
seek them, much less travel on them. I imagine, then, that it was because Asquith became
subject to the force of the high example spoken
of that he came to embrace 'Liberal Imperialist' doctrine, and, farther, so far discarded his
natural repugnance to war, its institutions and
'atmosphere,' and the life military in general,
as to accept Cabinet office in the capacity
mentioned, and even to glory in it, so far at
least as so cold a nature as his was capable
to feel so much satisfaction.

All life, from the first even to the last forms
of it, is subject to crisis. Birth is one, and
death comes to complete and crown the cycle;
but ever, 'twixt the two, occur others, which

make or mar us, give us fortune or destroy
our chances, according as we use them, or
peradventure neglect or fail to improve them
to our own advantage, as no doubt we might
and should do. The reader who is indulgent
already by nature will surely pardon these
platitudes, when he comes to learn that here
they appear merely to serve for introduction
to some observations I wish to make touching
Asquith, and Asquith's conduct, at the supreme
crisis of his political life; I mean, of course,
his quarrel with his fellow-minister, Lloyd
George.

If the modern version of the old Roman
tag that sought to oblige the living to speak
uniformly well of the dead were substituted
for the other, in this event, though such sub-
stitution might well please the taste of the
present age, yet exceptions to it in the shape
of persons there are, I doubt not, who would
be better pleased were the maxim wholly trans-
ferred to and applied to living men instead.
But in any event, it seems to me absurd practice to speak well of the dead merely because
dead they are; and, farther, practice as absurd
to speak well of the living simply because
alive they are. It must be plain indeed to
any man of sense that what should be spoken

is, of the dead, good if they deserve it, but ill
if they have done that which is wrong: the living, on the other hand, should be treated with
equal candour, but perhaps with a trifle more
severity, should severity towards them be justi-
fied; since to them at least, though not to the
others, is time yet given to mend their ways,
to improve their manners, to reform their
morals.

But I do not propose a portrait of Mr. Lloyd
George by way of illustration to these remarks:
such has been drawn already, by one or two
hands; and I believe, too, that, observing, it
may be, the example of some old masters of
the brush, who have bequeathed to ourselves
and all posterity portraits of themselves painted
by themselves, himself has done some drawings
and sketches of Lloyd George, which, though by
no means finished pieces, or indeed intended for
such apparently, yet have considerable imaginative power, and no little sensitiveness of design.
Besides, to deal at any length with living figures,
as to condescend to much detail touching them,
would be entirely foreign to the plan and purpose of the present work; and for this reason
I regret much that all such portraiture must
be excluded from it, and but the briefest men-
tions of living persons and their actions—and

such only when and where there is a positive
need of them—admitted to it.

Among the several shining merits, and the
sundry solid accomplishments, of the English
people, hardly shall we find, I imagine, the gift
of tongues, or yet among them much understanding of the natures of other races. The
gift I mention is useful to the people that has it,
since, speaking generally, it enables this people
to get into *rapport*, as it were, with foreigners
a deal more easily, and to better purpose,
than would be the case should they lack it.
This, I think, is plain, and what is surely no
less so is this, namely, that presuming this
gift or capacity of tongues on the part of a
people, such is good enough *prima facie* reasoning that, through the same channel, it should
come to a better understanding of its neighbours' natures, and reach this end much more
quickly, gifted as I have presumed this people
to be, than would be the case were it not so
favoured of God. On the other hand, if we
suppose a people that has no gift of tongues
to speak of, nor yet is much concerned to all
appearances whether it have it or no, in this
event it is little probable that this people will
take much interest in the affairs of its neighbours, or be at any pains to learn how their

minds work relatively to its own, and even what is passing among them.

It happened that long before Mr. Lloyd George came to make much figure in English political life, he was the subject of consider- able speculation in Ireland and Scotland, parti- cularly, I think, in the latter, where he soon became known to many as *Gille nan Car*, which means, interpreted, the 'Lad of the Tricks' or Stratagems. But the English, one of whose natural advantages or one of whose natural disadvantages is, that they are very apt to presume that all who enter their public life are of a temperamental piece with themselves, and who think, farther, that all who so join themselves to them, no matter what their origin by way of race, are necessarily bound by the same conventions, the same standards, and the same rules of conduct in political life, as they themselves observe, would not appear to have given much heed to this immigrant son of St. David at this early stage of his public career; but, on the contrary, accepted him, like the rest, for what they took him to be, that is to say, yet another ordinary recruit to their political arms and the civil life of the country.

It happened, farther, that when the great

crisis of Asquith's public career occurred, it came to him in the shape of Mr. Lloyd George. He never understood him, no matter how much he may have sought, or appeared to seek, his friendship, or the other may have sought, or appeared to seek, that of Asquith. They had different, and irreconcilable, natures; and what drove Asquith from office, broke his career, and has clouded his memory ever since, is this clash of two opposite natures, and its effects as they regard the subject of this sketch.

To say, as some alleged at the time, and have asserted since, that Asquith was cast out of office in the year 1916 because he failed to understand, or understanding, failed to press as was fit, the grave necessity of more and better arms and munitions of war generally, is, as it seems to me, silly talk—but child's babble. He was as much alive to this necessity and the supreme importance of it—and the fact can be proved with ease from the political correspondence, as well private as public, of those times—as were Mr. Lloyd George and the rest of the heads of the administration which was then in power; and for my part, I share the opinion of those who believe that, had Asquith been suffered to remain in office, he would have done as well in it at least as his supplanter came to do in it, if not better. He was a patriotic Englishman of great ability, trained in the English way to 'business' and long used to it; resolute, incorruptible, fearless, honest, and far-seeing: it is absurd to advance that such an Englishman was not as well fitted in every way to get his countrymen out of the mess they were in as was the little attorney from Wales.

But in the event it happened that Asquith was hustled out of office, because his nature was not capable to understand, or yet to withstand, that of his adversary, Lloyd George. I have said 'hustled' out of office of a purpose; for such was precisely the mode of expulsion applied to him at the time, particularly by some about him, and in public places, who conspired to 'beat him up,' in a political way, much as street-corner 'roughs,' and other base fellows of the town, intimidate, bewilder, and do violence to their prey. He succumbed to Lloyd George because he was confused, dazzled, bemused, and even to some extent hypnotized by the other's gifts, in respect of some of which he was himself by no means strong, at all well founded; such, for instance, as the power to excite enthusiasm in multitudes, to draw to himself clients and supporters in public life, to stir up emotion in the breast of the masses by means of wild harangue and declamatory speech, to generate promises easy to be replaced by others yet larger, more gaudy and alluring, should these others fail, which experience shows that they are uncommonly apt to do.

He saw intrigue approach, and make ready to strike; but his own attitude in face of it resembled that of a bird or other creature of the wild, which, fascinated, observes, all-powerless, the coming of its enemy. He did not witness the coming of his political death as Tully witnessed the advent of the wretched scrivener who was sent to slay him. The hour of collision came, and his was the career that 'crashed': he fell from the height of power, headlong, somewhat ineptly, but pitiably; and entirely unnecessarily, as it seems to me. In fine, the 'flabby part' of Asquith's nature was the weakness that he showed with respect to Lloyd George; just as, according to Sheridan, the 'flabby part' of Thomas Erskine's nature was the fear he had of the younger Pitt.

Still, Time, in whose hand are the scales of all earthly values, will weigh, with practised eye and hand, in after years, this man, whose worth posterity will know and prize, though to his parts and memory this age hesitates to

do full justice, and thus its duty by him.
For, despite the coldness of his gifts and
nature, the punctilios and refinements that,
taking their rise from his calling, marked his
conduct often, his Whiggishness, and somewhat
bourgeois views of men and things, and life
in general, Henry Asquith was a great Englishman—perhaps the last, though not the least, of
his country's ancient line of native statesmen.

CHARLES STEWART PARNELL

CHAPTER V

CHARLES STEWART PARNELL

I SUPPOSE that each of us has his or her
proper niche in the vestibules of the universal
order of the human world, that is to say, in
the general scheme of things; the plain intention of this being to adjust, to fit us, to circumstance, to the end that we may be useful
to society and God's purpose in founding it,
with as little hindrance, as slender interruption,
as may be.

But, most unfortunately, it happens often that
the particular niche made for us in life and
society is never filled by us. We prefer,
or at least somehow come to occupy, some
other; or, even whilst yet we hesitate, someone else springs up nimbly, and fills the niche
designed for us, and so in this way, or in the
other mentioned, circumstance is changed for
us or we ourselves take it into hand to alter it.

With the eye, as it were, of the dispensation
glanced at above, I seem to see at this moment
the subject of this sketch, niched, not as

Nature proposed, but as Charles Stewart Parnell willed and devised. I see him with the same eye in the act of leaning over a five-barred gate to an Irish field, with a straw in his mouth, and he conversing with a neighbour of the state of the weather, of markets, and agricultural matters and interests generally. In fine, it appears that Parnell's true avocation was country-gentleman; but then what happened was that fate, or some contrariety or exercise of the will, on his part, drew, or threw, him into politics.

I imagine he had not much natural talent for these: it does not follow always, much less often, that the line of life which a man chooses for himself is the line that he is best fitted for in respect of his temper, or by way of his talent, or yet by reason of both. Thus, for the ambidexterity of man due allowance must be made always; and, besides, there is ever our own blindness, and our forwardness to occupy situations which are truly nowise suited to us. His talent, then, was probably never profound, and politics, considered as a science, alien to him; but yet considered as party-leader he was, in his own person, no mean achievement, as thirty years and more of strict personal rule, which is about what his followers in the House

of Commons experienced of him, prove plain
enough.

I first met Parnell after the divorce, when
all but a few of his former political friends
and associates were fled, some, conscientiously
enough, on this account; but others not so
conscientiously: for private reasons of spite
and jealousy or party causes of hate; and
when, too, with back to wall, he was making,
but with no great success, the one great personal political fight of his life.   It happened on
the way to Roscommon; and the train was black
with his yelling supporters, much as one may
see bees that are on swarm clustered about a
branch; so that now was real danger to human
life, at the going in, and the going out, of the
train at the different stations we passed through,
on our royal road to Roscommon.

Thus I did not make Parnell's acquaintance,
or come to know him, till towards the close
of his political career and life; which some may
think a disability in my regard; now that, so
many years after his decease, I think to give
some of my thoughts touching him; but then,
in my opinion, in this view of matters is more
plausibility than actual truth.   Obviously a
man may know another in a few hours, if not
minutes, better than yet another man may

know the same individual though he come to
spend with him the whole of his lifetime.
There is even such a thing as flash-light in-
tuition, that is, instantaneous pure knowledge,
which, in the coming and going of less than a
second of time, illumes to us, suddenly, and as
searchingly as can be, the whole scene, as it
were, of a man's or a woman's moral nature.
But apart from these aids to our knowledge of
different men and women there is moral crisis,
under stress of which, as it commonly happens,
one man is apt to reveal his strength, and yet
another his weakness, but almost all men their
true character. Now Parnell was passing
through a crisis, and the crisis itself was more
than commonly pressing and testing when first
I became acquainted with him; and according
as the crisis developed with regard to him, so it
came to draw out from him his true nature,
and, by consequence, for me it multiplied
good occasions and opportunities of observing
and knowing him.

I have remarked already that probably Parnell
had no great genius for politics; but most
certainly he had none whatever for public
speaking. He had no gift of oratory, or care,
or understanding apparently, as to what eloquence consists in, theoretically or positively.

I remember one day: I heard him speaking in the open air, when, all of a sudden, the halting and laboured utterance ceased. One or two of the reporters, seated at a table in front of him, cast their eyes heavenwards, wishing no doubt for the missing word as eagerly as Paul on shipwreck wished for the day; and yet another that I knew slightly, tapping his teeth with his pencil, glanced my way with a smile, and winked, as though he should say: 'Wait till the miracle occurs, and this manna descends.' At long last, however, the absent word turned up, whereupon the whole speech rumbled on again, reminding me in that instant of some ancient diligence or stage-coach that, with much groaning of body and creaking of wheel, starts off on its travels. Perhaps the double paradox consisting in an Irishman that had not the gift of the gab, and an Ireland that listened to him long and eagerly, though much endowed with this gift, is best explained by the presumption of Ireland itself as land of paradox, and the nation that inhabits it for people given to acting the pun in a political way.

Still, though a man should have no great genius for politics subjectively considered, nor care, nor know, anything about statesmanship, the theory of it, its science, arts, and practices,

yet such a person can be a very good party
leader; and sometimes, too, so he is. Parnell,
though he knew and cared nothing about the
theories and science of statesmanship, yet was a
good party leader, as well as a political organ-
izer of parts. His interest in, and knowledge
of, agricultural matters in his own country
appeared very plainly, and to great advantage,
in all that he worked with regard to the Land
League, and the carrying on the agitation that
began the business of undermining English rule
in Ireland. In respect of 'practical' politics
of the sort glanced at he was eminent; and no
one who knows the almost incredible sloth of
his nature, and the inveteracy of his habit of
postponing to some other season the thing—
no matter what it might be—that needed to be
done *instanter*, or at all events most timeously,
but will be filled with admiration when he
comes to consider the way in which, in this
particular province at least, Parnell denied
himself, and set with success at defiance the
whole cast and temper of his mind.

I have said already that the cause, as the
occasion, of my coming to know Parnell was
the crisis that took place in his political affairs
after O'Shea divorced his wife, which took
him out into the country, there to do battle

with his political enemies for his political life.
The two Redmonds were with him at the time,
and some others that yet remained faithful to
him, and subject to his leadership, but whose
honest names I have forgot at the moment.
Now the great man was used to relax after he
and his political associates had dined; and it
was then more particularly that Parnell would
open his mind, and speak to the company with
perfect candour. I respected at the time, and
think that some respect should be paid to them
yet, these postprandial political confidences;
but I see no good reason why some at least of
them should not be broached, now that the
author of them is long in his grave, and the
circumstances under which they were given to
the few that heard them are entirely passed.
He was used then to make no secret of the
fact that the 'constitutional' agitation for Home
Rule in which the parliamentary party of
Ireland was engaged was but a pretence, in
the sense that the true design of the whole
national movement was absolute independence.
Avowals of policy and the like, made in one
set of circumstances, and considered at the time
as remarkable, sensational, or even dangerous
to be uttered, are very apt to fall flat when,
long after the time of their making, they become

generally known; when the circumstances in which they were made are no longer what they were originally; and so I suppose that Parnell's declaring in private for absolute independence at a time when he was forward to give out in public that he was but thinking 'constitutionally' with regard to Ireland and her political future will not much move the present reader, who has witnessed, probably, the Sinn Fein movement, and the establishment of a free state in a part of Ireland. But in those days it was tremendous; and, had it been declared, would have set all political England in a fury, I imagine.

To put ourselves with ease, with entire success, in the room of others is a moral feat as hard, I suppose, as any that can be, if indeed it be not harder even than the seeming hardest: at all events, I judge that so it is, by reason of the extreme infrequency of its occurrence. I say that for individuals to do this is extremely hard; but then for aggregates of them, in the shape of societies and peoples, it is impossible seemingly; and few of either kind or order are farther from it, I imagine, than the English, who give too much attention to sport, and other activities of the kind, to devote to it the thought that is necessary in order to its acquisition. The Englishman seems to think that he, his rule, his civilization and his culture are sufficient unto all that are nct of his own blood over whom he has established his sway; and, farther, he seems to resent, as being conduct contrary in some sort to the order of nature, and even morally wrong, any appearance of general dissatisfaction with his rule; and yet more strongly, and more particularly of course, any visible sign of revolt from it, of rebellion raised in order to make an end of it—whether by means of arms or otherwise matters not, seemingly.

This is, perhaps, the capital political vice of the Englishman, and what renders him unpopular abroad; but at the same time I allow very freely that it is what keeps together—far more and better than 'the golden link of the Crown,' on which the politicians of the nation are fond to expatiate at times—the empire which John Bull has managed to collect and establish, in the course of the later centuries. For not only does the feeling spoken of serve well to bind the English together, to encourage one and all of them to regard the empire they have formed as something above the common accidents of time and space, and therefore in some sort imperishable, yet some there are, but not of their own blood and country, who, seduced by the common example to the same way of thinking, are become as great sticklers for English rule and English empire as are the English themselves; and besides are very apt to turn on their own nationals, who think differently on this head, with the same severity as the English are wont to use with regard to them, being more forward to put them down, to stamp out dissatisfaction among them, than are their political pastors and masters of the Anglo-Saxon race.

Parnell knew this as well as he knew the buttons on his coat; and, being nationally-minded to the full, accordingly he understood the danger to his country, to the cause of national freedom, by reason of it, and made those declarations in private which he judged it impolitic at the time to make in public. Another truth, which was as plain to him as the other, is that, in this matter, the obligation, the *onus probandi* as it were, lies, as it has ever lain, on the Anglo-Irish—just as, in similar case, it continues to lie on the Anglo-Scot and the Anglo-Welshman—since the sort of politics which these political half-breeds profess, and stand for, are not those of the nations to which they belong, but alien views, and, what is more, views of recent appearance, and indefensible in a point of view of history and tradition. Thus Parnell was ever particularly *searbh* on his Anglicized countrymen, regarding them with the greatest dislike and contempt, though I never observed that he spoke with any considerable heat touching the English as a race: what he objected to, and objected to reasonably enough as it seems to me, was the presence of their rule in Ireland.

Someone once asked me if I knew the secret of the hold on his parliamentary followers which Parnell had, and exerted, too, on occasions, in a very odd manner; but I replied that, for my part, I thought there was no mystery or secret at all about the matter. When Parnell succeeded Butt in quality of leader to the Irish parliamentary party, he succeeded, at the same time, to the government of a thoroughly disciplined party. Thus his sway over them was in a manner by virtue of established axiom, that was automatic, even 'inevitable' by nature; and so did not take its rise, as some have supposed, from the leader's personal qualities, such as exceptional firmness of purpose, strength of will, and a dictatorial cast or habit of mind, which also have been ascribed to him, though very erroneously, I imagine. And I think that the justness of this view of the matter is proved well enough by what took place when the great 'split' occurred, and the men who had elected him to office, deserting him, caballed together in order to expel him from it. In that crisis of his political fortunes, all the bands of party discipline were loosed, and Parnell was discovered to the world naked, as it were, bereft of all the signs and symbols of the authority that had been bestowed on him, not, I repeat, for personal reasons, but because, to his electors at least, he seemed to be the best man available, the fittest to lead them and their cause to victory. It pleased a part of the press at the time, and it has pleased some biographers since, to make of Parnell a kind of mystery-man, a portentous and a riddle-like sign in the firmament of contemporary British politics, endowing him with qualities drawn from such famous figures as Sulla, Cavour, and Metternich, and rolling the abstract so begotten into one supreme person, the ex-leader of the Irish parliamentarians; but surely no one looking straight into the rather ordinary Anglo-Norman countenance of Charles Stewart Parnell, and gifted with a sense of values in human nature, could make so great mistake as this. He was very friendly to me, and gave me whilst I was

with him and his colleagues, on the occasion
mentioned, many opportunities of observing
him, of studying his character, of forming just
notions as to the qualities of his mind and
heart; but even so it never struck me for a
moment that he was in any way extraordinary,
an epoch-making figure, comparable, for instance, to Nicolò Machiavelli, or even to any
of the lesser lights of the Paduan school of
medieval politics.

It seems to me—and this is a thing that I
have touched formerly but make no apology
for touching again—that human greatness is
susceptible to be divided into two parts or
orders. There is, first, direct greatness, which
springs from the fount of human nature itself,
and in a manner is independent, as regards its
constitution and its achievements, of adventi-
tious circumstance, that is, of the particular
road or channel into which this great talent is
directed, and through, and by means of which,
it shows itself to the world. The second is
indirect greatness, and may be compared to
one who, stepping forth from his porch into
the sun's light at his time of going down, is
flooded with his ray, by which means he is
made splendid, is glorified — for a while at
least—out of all semblance to his true self.

What greatness was given to Parnell was of the second quality or order. The sun of the cause he served shone on him in that moment of time which we call 'life'; and he was in some sort transfigured; but, after all, borrowed lights, like borrowed plumes, fill no eye that looks to the soul and the mind of a man, and not to appearances — to the trappings and externals that often come to pass with presumed, but unverified, human greatness.

Still, 'as long as wave shall beat on shore,' and that, I suppose, is long enough for any taste, the name of Charles Stewart Parnell will occur with honour in the annals of his native land, yea—even though the word which is Tradition forget, and a yet greater fate neglect, him.

LORD GRANVILLE

CHAPTER VI

LORD GRANVILLE

I WAS standing in a doorway of the ball-
room of a country house many years ago
when, of a sudden, I heard a voice behind
me, which said, 'Come! I want to introduce
you to Lord Granville.' I turned, and saw my
father. I followed him, who took me to my
lord, who was standing at the time by himself
in another part of the ball-room; and I was
introduced to him. I had expected that my
father would remain by my side to help me to
sustain with credit the burden of this encounter;
but a glance I now shot his way showed me that
he was gone. I was very young at the time,
and straightway the several things which, as I
followed in my sire's wake, I had thought to
say to the great man, suddenly departed my
head, were dissipated, like vapour from the
spout of a boiling kettle. I was smitten tongue-
tied, and felt myself to grow red of face, all
too conscious that I must appear not one fool
but a series of them, and each greater than the

other. Observing my confusion, says my lord to me very kindly, 'I hope you will come to see us in London'; and at this I murmured my thanks, bowed, and withdrew.

In after days I was often at Lord Granville's pleasant house in Charles Street. It still stands, I think, though near all the rest of the true West End of London has been pulled down by Israelitish builders with a craze for 'flats' —the noisiest and most inconvenient type of residence that can be. His house was practically in Berkeley Square, the east side of which, however, is no longer private dwellings, but a sort of bazaar, in which you may see poulterers, vendors of furniture, the signs of house-agents and lawyers, and other intruders of the kind, profaners of soil that at one time was held sacred to the foot of Mayfair. Said a house-agent to me lately, to whom I had grumbled touching this melancholy state of affairs, 'It is Progress!' saying this with the air of one who invokes a god: as if it were conclusive of the whole matter. But then neither this poor man, nor yet the multitudes of his kind who hold similar language to-day, appear to have taken the least trouble to analyse the sense of the remark; for in the notion of 'Progress' is contained very obviously a double principle of change, that

is, a contingency of good, and a contingency
of change towards ill; and, besides, a utilitarian
purpose and yet an aesthetic motive; and
'Progress' positive immediately calls these
qualities into operative being. On this reasoning, then, simply because it occurs, 'Progress'
is by no means necessarily such in the vulgar
sense of the word; and it is only by means of
a careful balance of the advantages and the
disadvantages of it that it is possible to determine whether any particular change is principally good or, on the other hand, principally
evil; and there I beg leave to leave this matter in
the meanwhile.

To the faces of several houses in the habit-
able parts of London are affixed circular blue
earthenware plaques, telling the passer-by that
'in this house' lived formerly some famous
man or other; but I observe that no such
commemorative plaque has been affixed to the
face of the house in Charles Street in which
Lord Granville and his lady lived for a number
of years. Yet hard by, in Grosvenor Square,
to be precise, is a house on which is a plaque
that tells us that here another diplomat, to wit
Walter Hines Page, from the United States of
America, resided for a while. It reminded
me, who had forgotten it, that this gentleman

was ambassador to England during the whole
of the late war; and I have collected since
that he was a voluminous writer of letters,
some of which are published in the form of a
book; but a book, I feel sure, which none reads
nowadays, if any besides a handful of reviewers
read it at the time; and even these few read it
but perfunctorily, I suppose, since the collec-
tion I refer to is dull as dull can be. I know
not who determines these things—the setting
up the plaques, I mean—but it seems to me odd
in the highest degree that while the memory
of this very inconsiderable American diplomat
should be honoured with a commemorative
plaque in Grosvenor Square, Lord Granville's
should be, so far, plaqueless in Charles Street.
Is this, I ask, yet another illustration of the
English national disinclination, or inability, to
think rationally, or, on the other hand, are
we to regard it as one of many instances of
make-believe, in respect of which the English
excel, when the object of it is their 'cousins
across the sea'; and the political occasion presses
them to it?

This waywardness, this capriciousness, in
respect of the affixation of commemorative
plaques to houses, is, I suppose, a consequence
in some sort of the spiritual motions, in the

spaces of men's minds, of the common notions
as to finite fame; and so these plaques might
be related, with perfect propriety, to such
similar objects as public statues, and other
commemorative emblems of the kind, which
are used to be erected, like the others, very
capriciously, though of course in far greater
profusion; my own private humble opinion
being that all these different commemorative
activities want the precision, the certainty,
and the co-ordination which, in respect to
their incidence, they lack most evidently, because we have no sure means to determine
fame, no fixed standards by which it might
be measured and cast off, as it were, in
commemorative form. We labour under the
same difficulty, and by consequence are in the
same uncertainty, when we come to determine
poetry, indeed the 'values' of the arts generally;
and, farther, I suppose that a more searching,
if not a more captious, opinion would be that
the whole civilized world is infirm, and ever
has been so, for precisely the same reason,
that is to say, because sure fixed standards are
everywhere wanting to us, humanly speaking.
But be this particular matter as it will, I have
no doubt whatever that there was more true
diplomacy in a single formal diplomatic script

of moment of Lord Granville's than can be found in the whole mass of documents uttered by this same Walter Hines Page.

We date the modern world, and in so dating we time its birth, reasonably enough no doubt, from the Renaissance. In early medieval times the principal diplomats were churchmen, and especially the higher ecclesiastics. Kings, princes, and civil magistrates generally, had not then much education, which was engrossed to the Church, and despised rather than sought and honoured by the others. Some of these bishops and other great churchmen were notable diplomats; but it should seem that what science they, as such, had, has perished in their company. The two great founders of modern diplomacy were Nicolò Machiavelli and Francesco Guicciardini, from whose writings it is possible to collect a whole science of it.

Both these men were historians, and both diplomats. The first wrote a history of Florence, and the second did the same, as well as a general history of Italy. Both therefore, since the three works mentioned are commonly, and justly, reckoned great history, were well grounded in 'business,' as politics were styled in that age, and continued to be so styled till about the middle years of the eighteenth

century. Scattered through these pages are
much sound counsel and lively and pertinent
remark touching the conduct of business,
and the handling the great men that have
authority in states, the younger doctor, namely
Guicciardini, being perhaps the richer oracle
in these respects. And for my part I think
there is more to be learned touching the science
of diplomacy from the specifically historical
writings of these men than is to be collected
from either Nicolò or Francesco in their more
political advices, such as the *Discorsi* of the first,
or the *Ricordi Politici e Civili* of the second,
since maxim of the sort proffered in these two
works is apt to lose point and colour both,
when, as happens here, it is wrested as it were
from the text of the history which is its best
illustration.

Generally, both Machiavelli and Guicciardini
adhered to the notion that history repeats
itself, and farther, they believed that the essential qualities of man change not at all, nor have
changed at all *ab initio*. In other words,
their opinion was that there is a law of nature
which obliges itself to the repetition of itself
in respect of all its parts and activities—a very
plausible theory surely if regard be had to
the fact that all our measures of time repeat

themselves with unfailing regularity, that the son is but in some sort a repetition of the father, the daughter of the mother, and that sermons, speeches of all kinds, private conversations, and the arts are activities devoted very obviously to this particular principle. However, it is hardly to be believed that Machiavelli imagined, even for a moment of time, that this great law of nature was so punctual as to its occurrence, so absolute as to the execution of itself, that from it might be deduced with certainty an exact science of history, and, therefore, an exact science of diplomacy, though Guicciardini had the front to twit the other touching this very matter, in his *Discorsi Politici*, which is mainly a criticism of Machiavelli's opinions. It is plain that the repetition of father in son, of mother in daughter, is but a relative or approximate, and not an absolute one, within the bounds of human species; neither, too, it is plain, does history repeat itself absolutely; but with approximations only to former states, events, conditions, passages, and conjunctures. The conclusion, therefore, is irresistible, and this it is, namely, that there is not, nor can be, any such thing as an exact science of history; and since of the structure of the diplomatic craft or function maxim drawn from history is its principal part, neither here, too, where no true ground of it exists, can be, by any possibility, 'exactness.'

I have dwelt the longer on this point because, in England at least, little general esteem, and on the whole small understanding, are shown touching the function and profession of the diplomat. In the firmament of politics peculiar to it the diplomats themselves appear as stars that shine with a cold faint light, that are so far retired from earth into the remotest parts of the heavens as to be little objects of the popular astronomy. Indeed in this country there seems to be a general suspicion of both, which, I think, may be traced to two principal causes: the legend of Machiavelli, and popular jealousy.

With regard to the first matter, though it is true that the doctrine of this notable Italian did not begin to enter the political world generally till long after his writings were composed, and true also that, when at least it entered it, his doctrine was as generally misunderstood, yet undoubtedly the Florentine came to be suspected in proportion as he was studied, and disliked in the same ratio in which his name, if not his canon, became known. The extreme callousness and unrelieved brutality of some of his counsel, and the positive wickedness of certain of his applauded examples, united to cover his memory with infamy, and through this channel he besmirched the whole order, the entire race and profession, of the diplomat; for folk who had no knowledge of Machiavelli beyond his bare name were naturally forward enough to think and speak ill of him in particular, and the science of diplomacy in general, once that scholars, and other men of parts and learning, had digested him, had pointed out his offences against Christian ethic, and drawn attention to the important part he had played with regard to the refoundation of the calling to which he belonged. The bad parts of him were cried to the world; but the fair and the good neglected to be made known, or at least so much sunk as to be completely hid, to the popular view at least, beneath the others. That the Florentine has been the undeserving object of a wicked conspiracy to defame him everlastingly would be, I think, an absurd contention; but that he has been cursed to the skies without due regard to what is good in him, and diplomacy itself darkened with his shadow, this, I think, could be proved without the smallest difficulty.

With regard to the second matter, De Tocqueville remarked some time ago—in the last century, to be more precise—that a principal mark of a democracy is jealousy; and this axiom, I suppose, it should not be hard to establish, either before his day or since, by examples drawn from the old Greek republics, by that of medieval Europe, Florence, and the Italian democracies generally, down to our own times. The sovereign people is apt to be jealous even to a point of absurdity, touching the power and authority trusted to the civil magistrates it has itself appointed to rule over it; and to this feeling of jealousy is conjoined, very often, a strong and lively suspicion of all forms of state secrecy. The principles of the science of diplomacy are largely laid in this quality, and diplomats generally must practise it, even though they abstain from seeming to cultivate it for a habit. Among the several vain cries raised by the multitude at the outbreak of the late war was a cry for the abolition of 'secret diplomacy,' which, by virtue of a process of reasoning that remains as obscure as it was so originally, the democracy thought to be a capital cause of it. Every man of sense who is at all familiar with such diplomatic correspondence relating to the beginnings of the war as has been published in Europe since it was ended, will allow readily enough, I suppose, that *some* 'secret diplomacy' might well be a contributory, though yet but a secondary, cause of the war; but that diplomacy generally, *per se* as it were, which continues to use secrecy as much as it ever did, and must continue to use it as long as this science continues to be practised, was a principal cause of the war—this position, if assumed, is overthrown very easily, I think. I cite this instance (which I had not done in different circumstances) because I think it a good illustration as well of that open jealousy of authority, which democracies commonly show, as of that latent suspicion of secrecy working at the sources of government and civil rule which unite to render the profession of diplomacy unpopular with the people, and diplomats themselves objects of suspicion to it.

One day that I walked with Lord Granville in Hyde Park I asked him who, in his opinion, should be considered as the best diplomat of modern times. He hesitated a trifle before he replied to me: then said he: 'It is said that comparisons are odious; generally speaking, they are certainly hard to draw justly. One must remember, too, that formerly the diplomat enjoyed far more liberty of action than he does nowadays, when he is the servant, not of a single master, but of several, in the shape of a Cabinet, the members of which owe a collective responsibility, first to the sovereign, secondly to the party, and thirdly to the people who have placed this party in power; and that makes all the difference — to the diplomat, I mean. For instance, Cecil, who served Queen Elizabeth, and served her remarkably well, too, had but a single mistress to consult, and either because she trusted him fully, or felt herself unequal to dealing with the problems he had to deal with, the queen allowed him an entirely free hand. Such names as Richelieu, Mazarin, Metternich, and perhaps Talleyrand, immediately occur to me; but to distinguish between them in the sense your inquiry demands would need a very careful digest, and a long series of reasonings.'

Himself had so much the air of a diplomat that he might well have stood for model of one for the stage, or for the pages of a romance. He was uniformly urbane in his manner and extremely polite of speech; and if at times his smile seemed to be a little too obviously designed to create the impression on the part of the person on whom he used it that he held secrets of great price that must never be divulged, the stage-craft was pardonable enough: it was, in part at least, I think, a habit of countenance that grew in him in proportion as he made progress through this unconsciously amusing world. His deportment in the council chamber was ever as easy, as full of aplomb, as his carriage and conduct in social life were finished.

He was a great student of European history, and studied the whole science of 'business' with avidity, and a particular care. From both he drew to himself a body of principles, sufficient as to quality and quantity both, to render him illustrious in all time, had his application of these principles to the different circumstances and conjunctures with which he engaged during the course of his public career been firmer, less hesitating at times (and those the most critical ones) than it was. His whole mind, nature, and training were formed to diplomacy; for my part I think it a pity that he allowed, as undoubtedly he did allow, the distractions of party politics to divert him often from this principal purpose.

Lord Granville had what is commonly styled a 'distinguished career,' which means, I take it, that yet a little more talent, a trifle better conduct in it, would have made him enduringly illustrious. His capital fault was hesitancy, that is, want of moral power to apply, at critical times, with vigour, and possibly with ruth-

lessness, the principles wherewith he was fully
indoctrinated.

In one capacity or another, he passed through
successive Whig administrations, but always
drawing from them, as it seems to me, more
colour than he gave to them. He was little
use as a party-man or leader; so that it was well
for the Whigs that he stood down on one or
two occasions when the party call should have
been for him, rather than for the person who in
the event came to respond to this call, to take
place above Granville by reason of it. In the
capacity mentioned he did better in the Lords,
whose then air of other-world politics and stale
privilege was more congenial to his nature, and
so allowed better use of his talent.

It is plain that it would be impossible to
give in this place a detail of Lord Granville's
public career; and, besides, these 'portraits'
make no pretence to be more than sketches of
the different subjects that here appear. Few
lives, as it seems to me, deserve to be so de-
tailed; and, most certainly, that of my Lord
Granville is not one of them.

His principal performance in public life was,
I suppose, the laying of the foundations of
the political *entente cordiale* 'twixt this country
and France. He loved Paris and spoke French

supremely well. He had strong French sym-
pathies, which he showed very plainly, even
to the disgust of many of his countrymen,
when France and Prussia went to war. The
work mentioned was congenial to him, and
it was the kind of diplomacy, too, in respect
of which he was particularly well fitted. In
the armoury of his arts as a diplomat, urbanity,
gentle but astute persuasion, and what Matthew
Arnold styles somewhere 'sweet reasonableness'
—all directed to political ends—such, I say, were
his principal weapons; and these he used on the
occasion mentioned to such good effect that its
witness remains even to this day.

Another principal exploit of his occurred
when the Montenegrin question arose, one of
those minor problems of international politics
which intrigue, and the perversity of human
nature in high places, are apt to foment to
the general confusion. On the crested billows
of this troubled sea Granville poured with
entire success the tranquillizing oil of his diplomatic smile. The armed savages that are the
Great Powers of Europe laid aside their weapons
for a while, and peace that is ever the prelude
to war reigned over Europe once more.

But I find no element of human greatness in
Lord Granville, sure though I am that he was

a man of very considerable mental gifts. His
portrait is set here because I regard him as,
in some sort, among the last of a type, an
attractive survival into our times of a species
of administrative politician whose like was
much more forward in Renaissance days, and
immediately afterwards, because it was far
better suited to them, than it has been since
either forward, or suited, to these. For types,
like the mortals of whom they are composed,
and whom they symbolize and represent, come
and go, flourish for a while, and then, after a
while, first of decline, and next of decay,
perish, and disappear.

ARTHUR JAMES BALFOUR

CHAPTER VII

ARTHUR JAMES BALFOUR

I FIRST made the acquaintance of the subject of this sketch on the doorstep of his own house in London. I had a letter of introduction to him, and was calling on him in order to leave it, when the encounter I speak of occurred.

Now, in my view of the matter at least, a doorstep is an awkward place for a meeting of the kind here glanced at. True, it is stone; but if stone yet as stepping-stone to friendship, or even common social commerce, I think it negligible, if not worse. Whether or no Mr. Balfour himself felt this, I cannot say for sure; but what I know for sure is that I felt it strongly at the time. It is singular how left-handed occurrences of this sort are apt to colour and condition, subsequently, our relations with our fellow-creatures. They are apt to run all through them, much as in some operas a short principal refrain is made to run through the entire piece.

He received me civilly enough, and invited me within. For a while, we talked of friends we had in common, and, *more Scotorum*, of families and their genealogies, till I raised the matter of philosophy, in which of course I knew him to be interested. I said that I had lately done some reading in the Scots school, meaning, not such minds as Barclay and Andrew Black, but the later sages, such as Hume, Ferguson, and others like to them. At once his mind reacted politically to these observations, and he remarked, with all the tartness that the Anglicized Scot is apt to use, when he fears, or at all events suspects, the near approach to him, in some way or form or other, of the bogy of the native nationalism, that we could 'no longer departmentize philosophy; since now the science is without national frontiers or racial quality of any kind.' I felt that I could not with reason allow him this position; and I said so, observing that it appeared to me that man was become the bubble of his own convention in the shape of time. 'What is there,' said I, 'in human knowledge or experience to prevent the appearance nowadays of a distinctively Scottish school of philosophy, presuming, of course, the existence of minds equal and formed to the undertaking I mention?

Nothing, that I can see' (I concluded), 'that was not already in existence at the time of the first, second, or third appearances of this school.' He did not reply; but looked at me a trifle more attentively than he had done hitherto. 'Are you interested in politics?' he said. I replied, 'Not in the least,' meaning that I was not interested in the sort of politics which he and his kind among my countrymen pursued. 'But' (I went on) 'I had a long conversation at the Foreign Office with your uncle last week.' 'Indeed,' says he; 'that at least must have interested you.' 'He was very kind' (I continued), 'and at the end of it he said that he would let me know if he heard of anything, though I had not come to solicit him in any way.' 'A mere formula,' said Balfour with a smile, and a wave of his hand. 'Probably his mind was already entirely detached when he repeated it, quite unnecessarily no doubt, to you.' And then he said a thing very true and striking, which I am much pleased to have an opportunity of setting on record here. 'It' (he meant the formula) 'is the bell that peals the birth, and sounds the knell at once, of youthful hope.' And so ended my first meeting with Arthur James Balfour.

Now if there be in time or space such an

entity as the genius of the Eldest Son—and I am inclined to think most strongly that this is so—in that event my belief is that A. J. Balfour had a deal of it. He was one himself; and had somewhat of the arrogance, the superciliousness, and the intellectual coxcombry— where intellect is present among them in any force, to any purpose—which commonly mark them, and is apt to render them odious and ridiculous to others. In the English social economy at least, The Eldest Son holds high hereditary office, and his lordship is used to be favoured with rich material on which to walk, in sharp contradistinction to· what happens to the opposite, yet complementary, entity: I mean of course The Younger Son, who, though he has a more interesting history than the other, a longer and more illustrious pedigree, and, in the gross, greater honours to his sort, yet in England at least is little considered, and as a rule worse rewarded, when he happens to do society some notable service.

Well, as I was about to remark, when this parenthesis overtook me, and led me astray for a while, Balfour's manner was often what might be described with perfect justness as 'unfortunate.' His general pose in life, and attitude towards his fellow-men, is symbolized

in some sort by some of the sketches of parliamentary scenes prepared by the late Harry
Furniss, and published in the press from time
to time in his day, in which the artist is fond
to represent the statesman as lolling in his seat
on the Treasury bench, with an air about him
of mixed boredom and superciliousness.   How
far the artist's ascription was true, because
proper to the nature of the subject of his
pencil, I am not, nor ever was, sure in mind;
but then if, as I suspect, art and affectation
were both strongly represented in Balfour,
such neither excuses it now, nor rendered it
then the less irritating to those who were the
objects of it.

Still, I allow very freely that Arthur Balfour
made a charming host—kind, courteous, considerate, and, on occasions, surprisingly tolerant to
all seeming, of opinions that must have grated
much with him, being indeed designed to
provoke him to those asperities of judgment,
and sarcasms of speech, to which he was prone,
and doubtless had given a loose to, in other
circumstances and occasions, and under different
conditions.

Most of us, I suppose, are vain by nature,
and in Balfour vanity took the form of a strong
belief on his part that not only was he intended

for philosophy, but was indeed a philosopher of parts. Whereas the truth of the matter is, I imagine, that nature intended no such thing in his regard, and, secondly, that neither art nor industry on his part could ever make him such. Deep and continuous thinking involves a severe physical strain on him who seeks to practise it. Near all the great thinkers in the philosophic line have been, to the best of my recollection and belief, men of great physique. Balfour had not this physical requisite; and though it is true that he came to live a deal longer than seemed at all probable, judging by his slender physique and ailing ways, yet he was ever delicate, ever prone to seasonal indisposition, and generally of a tender cast and type of body; and these physical weaknesses are reflected most plainly in his philosophic thought, which, to say truth, is, generally, shallow, superficial—creditable enough no doubt to a dilettante, such as he was, but entirely negligible as serious philosophy.

When the genius of Stevenson put the drama of Dr. Jekyll and Mr. Hyde on the stage of fiction, many thought the duality mighty surprising; but though, instead, he had multiplied this duality many times, and published the piece, it should not have occasioned the least

surprise to any one.   I confess I find it difficult
to fix as truly representative of his nature any
one of the several different Arthur Balfours
that I perceived, from time to time, in the
one visible and consolidated Balfour.   He was
versatile to profusion, and compound far above
the compound quality of most compounds;
and if this in some sort was his charm, also it
was his undoing as a public man.   He had, and
nourished, far too many whims, postures, and
poses, ever to be in any one particular, in
any one province, great or even very eminent.
In this regard he resembled Alberoni or the
Cardinal of Lorraine—disappointing figures of
history, because neither could ever be brought
to apply his talent to a single end.   These,
and other men like to them, resemble sandy
deltas which absorb to a great extent the waters
of the rivers that pass through them towards the
sea.   Such afford often fine scenery; but then
they are little like the rivers that pursue a single
well-marked course, with whole waters that run,
from source to mouth, deep and strong.

He rose from post to post, as such men in
general are apt to rise, with applause, but ever
with an air of not seeming to intend it; and
most certainly without doing anything extraordinary to mark his passage from one office

to another, or yet his tenure of any of these successive posts. His own party had nicknames for him, which were more familiar by nature than respectful to his situation, his pretensions, and his talent; and the common opinion of such as were not of his own party in the House of Commons seems to have been that though he was by no means what dealers style an 'exceptional piece,' yet he was a necessary principal part of the furniture of any Conservative Administration of those times.

He had much skill in dialectic, and turns of resource in debate that were sometimes surprising; yet, on the whole, his leadership of his party, when he came to lead it, was undistinguished, uneventful, and humdrum. I speak here relatively, of course—relatively to such leaderships as that of Disraeli, of Fox, of Pitt, of Chatham, and other brilliant performers in the line I speak of that I could mention, but see no need to do so.

Eels are elusive to the hand because of the slime that is on them, and sparrows, though they have tails, yet are hardly to be caught by means of placing salt on them. I wish much I could define Balfour more narrowly than, so far at least, I fear I have done; but always, and everywhere about him, one is baffled by the profusion of his nature and the transformations of his genius. I cannot so much as guess the model on which he formed himself, and set himself forward in the world, there to invite men's gaze, to call forth judgment touching him. Did he design to pass for a modern Henry St. John, or imitate Cecil or Strafford in the guise of the new species that entered the world of English politics with the passage of the Reform Bill? I cannot say. At times he seems to have proposed to himself for model Themistocles, otherwhiles Pericles, or the younger (and more tolerable) of the two Catos; but ever all was vague, clouded with uncertainty, wrapped in the mystery of his own conceit, his own infirmity of aim and purpose.

He had eloquence, and acquired art as regards the showing forth of it; but this Muse of his was not capable to the highest flights. Generally, his oracle lacked certainty, precision, virility, spaciousness, and resonance of thought: it smelled too strongly of the schools, that is, the little private debating societies, such as one finds at Oxford and similar seats of learning, and these he frequented much at one time.

Some men acquire with age qualities and natures of which their first youth, and even their middle life, afford little, if any, of the signs of existence in them; and often, when this takes place, though late, these figures come to take their proper place in the galleries of fame, and thus do they resemble in some sort autumn flowers, whose glory, like the Wine of Merit at the Marriage Feast, is reserved till late; but then such did not happen in the case of Arthur Balfour. From first to last, he was as a ship that ever preserves an even keel in a little-ruffled ocean; never far from land in the boldest course; her load but common merchandise, and her skipper bound by owner's orders to sail for safety always, and avoid adventure. When in the year 1906 he resigned the leadership of his party, he withdrew from it as quietly, with as little ceremony and as scant applause, as a pilot leaves the ship he has been called to sail to port; and he was as little missed apparently by his fellow-Tories, and the English political world in general, as the other is missed—when he, too, retires — by the vessel's company. Seemingly, it is of the nature of man's genius, and human kind in general, that the dead are seldom mourned long: the grave closes over them as completely as the sea, or the waters of loch or river, closes over the object that is dropped into it, and even the richest men alive are not long missed when they come to die, in witness of the truth of which observation I cite Midas, and Croesus, and Crassus—familiar household names, perhaps, even to this day, but now long cut off by time, the popular forgetfulness, and the public ignorance of and indifference to history, from all true connection with their proper stories.

As to talent, and extraordinary merit generally, if, in the shape of the persons of deceased exemplars of either or both, the latter receive burial at all, it is in a pauper's grave, and not in a gilded mausoleum, erected at the public expense, and amid the general applause, that these honourable remains are too often laid. Hardly did Arthur Balfour deserve a public funeral when he came to die; but the extreme indecency of the haste with which the age that witnessed him has buried his memory since, must shock for sure every right-thinking man. Without a doubt, a part of the oblivion that has befallen him already, he drew on himself whilst yet he was alive: another part of it is due to the slenderness of his performance, considered in the gross; and yet a third consists in a quasi-self-protective motive, that is, the old demand of 'present' of 'past' that it should bury its dead as expeditiously as may be. Still, when every allowance which the nature of

the occasion requires to be made shall have
been made, and we are free, by consequence,
to proceed to judgment as to this matter,
it will be seen, and felt very poignantly and
generally, I imagine, that the soul of Arthur
Balfour has far less cause to rejoice as it marches
on through the maze-like vestibules of specu-
lative philosophy, towards a less perplexed
and more intelligible place of domicile, than
many another, who was far less talented, far less
favourably circumstanced, and far less highly
placed on earth than he was, enjoys, but who,
like him, and countless others, marches on from
the ends of time, through the middle-world,
towards eternity.

Grammarians are useful to language, and
might be so, at least on occasions, to writers
(especially to such of them as compose nowadays in English), one would think; but no
doubt the professional jealousy and disdain
of these arid pundits prevents the tolerance
spoken of: statisticians are folk who labour in
the mines of social undertakings of all sorts,
and send up to earth the malleable material
they find there, whose ready market is the
publicists who deal with the controversial
questions of the hour; and these are much
more esteemed than the others mentioned.

Yet a third class of social providers—extremely useful, too, in their way—consists in another kind of miners who, descending into the bowels of libraries, and places of deposit of old writings and documents, search them for the jewels of fact and fancy which they think lie hidden there, and returning to the surface, such as have them trade them to historians and biographers, who buy them eagerly, and use them to adorn their pages. I think I am betraying no great trade secret when I say that each and every 'well-documented' history and biography that appears in our day is in some sort the effect of the labours of these industrious and useful servitors to letters.

The design of these few observations should be plain, I suppose. In any event, their purpose is to introduce a notion that, centuries hence, peradventure someone or other belonging to the class of diggers last mentioned may be the means of rediscovering to his age and the world in general Arthur James Balfour; and should that happen which, all things considered, I think very like to happen, in that event the subject of this sketch should enjoy, being dead, much better fame and fortune than he enjoyed in life, or has, in the meanwhile. Disinterred as it were, it may well fall out that the statue of him cast for one of the several halls of the English national Valhalla will be of an heroic, instead of a natural, size; for it appears that as in autumn the shadows lengthen, so sometimes do these others grow in our esteem, in proportion to the distance 'twixt their day and ours.

The common place of burial for what Boling-broke styles somewhere 'the lumber of every administration, the furniture of every court, that is to say, secondary political talent of all kinds,' is county histories, peerages, dictionaries of biography, etc., and in these restful and se-cluded quarters the dead lie thick as fallen leaves, and in perfect peace, little like to be disturbed till the great last Trump shall sound, and the living and the defunct be gathered together to judgment. A man of my acquaintance that once held Cabinet rank, but, coming to retire from the administration in which he had sat, re-ceived a peerage of his king—this man, I say, fell upon a singular device when, his end approach-ing, he perceived that now naught but the grave and oblivion awaited him. He was a merchant by trade, and passed his whole life in London, knowing no more probably about husbandry and country-life and such matters in general than might be collected from a contemplation of the

vegetables in a greengrocer's, or the corn in a
corn-chandler's, shop-window. Yet he bought
an estate; and, retiring into the country, when
he came to die he left directions that his coffin
should be taken to the grave in an ordinary farm-
cart, drawn by oxen, or it might be horses, for
as to this latter point my memory fails me somewhat. Still, if in this case the matter of the por-
terage remains obscure, yet the agriculturist's
intention, though but symbolically expressed,
is plain enough: it was, no doubt, so to devise
the way and manner of his departure from
life as to cheat fate and convention of some
part at least of the customary mortuary dues,
to escape the doom of the oblivion that is apt
to fall on such as are distinguished by reason
of the honours and the riches which they have
gained for themselves in the course of their
labours through this world, but at the same
time are not otherwise celebrated. Doubtless
time alone can show whether or no the per-
petrator of this ingenious pleasantry was justi-
fied at the hour of his death of his resource
and sagacity, his foresight and extreme invent-
iveness of mind.

On the whole matter, then, the solemn conclusion to which I am come is, that in Arthur
James Balfour was no principle or element of

human greatness, though I allow, freely enough, that he was talented much above the common, and, farther, that at one time he rose high as high can be in the public councils of the English nation. His portrait is set among the others here collected, because he seems to me, collectively considered as it were, to illustrate a negation—perhaps even a series or succession of them—in talent, the general effect in life of which always is—no matter whether it occurs singly, by the dozen, or in massed formation— to restrict the mind, cripple the endeavours, limit the performance, and even impair the character, of the person in whom the disability I speak of appears.

LORD ROSEBERY

CHAPTER VIII

LORD ROSEBERY

OF the different 'little actors' that appear on the stage of history from time to time, and act a part there, which, though not considerable, yet is often interesting, the dilettante, considered as a sort of lesser social institution, deserves some mention, some notice proportioned to the figure he cuts, the part he plays. In the histories of all the nations of the West, traces, now lively, now but faint, of the dilettante, and, consequently, of the peculiar cult associated to him in the common mind, appear; and though no doubt the traces spoken of become a deal more plain to view, and much more numerous, too, after the revival of learning than they were so before the event I speak of occurred, yet, even in the earliest times, were dilettanti—among the Celts of Gaul and Britain, among the warring septs and tribes of Italy, in Spain; and earlier still of course at Rome, and, earlier yet, in Hellas.

It should seem, however, that no matter how

familiar this name may be to us, and how often it may occur in history, or appear in modern life and letters, it is but seldom strictly defined, and but rarely employed with propriety. Accordingly, with or without the reader's permission, I propose to devote a few words to it, not, I hasten to add, because I am so foolish, so entirely presumptuous, as to imagine that I alone possess the true science of this matter; but because I think it needs defining anew, fixing, as to the sense of it, as I suppose it was fixed when first it appeared among us.

Following former custom, then, I should distinguish the dilettante from the amateur by saying that, whereas the latter is but a casual or at best but a half-time patron and practiser of the arts, the former is a whole-time practiser in this respect. Indeed, often the amateur is but his own patron, as it were; and this, I think, is particularly true of him to-day, when all purses, save a few, are shrunk indeed, and men of letters, and others who follow the calling of the arts, starve by the thousand. Whereas, presuming that men like Cosmo and Lorenzo de Medici, or even Maecenas, who, however, would not appear to have practised that which his profusion endowed on so many and notable occasions—for which reason

I am a little slow to mention him in this connection—still, if these men and their like were
susceptible to be found among us to-day, in that
event I doubt not they would be as generous to
the arts, as forward to help struggling talent, as
were any of that figure in history.

Again, the amateur is but a dabbler in the
arts; whereas he cannot be a true dilettante
that does not devote his whole life to them, no
matter whether he never writes a line, handles
a brush, strikes a note, or takes up mallet and
chisel; for the essence of the true dilettante is
not practice of the arts (which many dilettanti
had done a deal better to avoid altogether), but
entire devotion to the cause of art.

Amateur talent (no matter what form it may
take) that is applied to the arts is often respectable enough; and farther, that amateurs there
are who, each in his chosen province, excel
some, if not all, professionals as regards the
practice of the arts—this surely is true enough.
Still, speaking generally, bad art is amateur
art. When we say that such and such a piece
is 'amateurish,' we mean that it is very far
from being perfect; and the slight or slur so
cast on it is sufficient indication as to the nature
of the opinion which the world in general
holds—and justly enough, experience tells us—

touching amateurs and the visible effects of such art as they may practise.

Distinguishing now the dilettante from the amateur who but dabbles in art, and spends his leisure, in part at least, by flirting with it more or less seriously, the first is to be understood as devoting his whole life and talent (and perhaps his whole fortune also) to it. A good example in England of the sort of person I mean is Horace Walpole: Scotland I shall deal with in a little more detail when I come to the subject of the present sketch —Lord Rosebery.

Walpole had parts, and wealth, too, sufficient of the latter at least to support with credit, though not with that splendour of profusion which the family of De Medici showed in Italy, the state to which he came by choice, in which he continued all through his natural life, and which in some sort he adorned. He was always curious as to the practice and progress of the arts; this curiosity he showed not only historically but as regards his own country and abroad. He cultivated a large private correspondence with persons eminent in letters, in painting, music, architecture, and sculpture; and with many others who, in these islands or elsewhere, were distinguished by reason of

the love and understanding they had of the
fine arts, and polite pursuits in general. Himself might not be much of an author, though
he wrote a deal (which, however, is little read
nowadays) on the topics that more particularly
interested him, with considerable learning,
though with no great originality or depth and
acuteness of judgment. In fine, I think Walpole
as fair a definition of the word dilettante as
can be had, as good an example of the institution itself as appears anywhere in English
history since the revival of learning towards
the close of the Middle Ages. His match, and
perhaps more than his match in some respects,
has appeared since the period I name in other
European republics of arts and letters, in
France and Germany, in Spain and Italy, for
instance; but these matters I must leave to
other hands to deal with.

In Scotland, where is a long and full tradition of culture, I need not go any higher in
history than the reign of James III, though I
had much liked, had theme and time and space
but permitted it, to say something here touching the first of the two revivals of learning
that have happened in Europe within historic
times; I mean, of course, that great flowering
of the Celtic culture which, begun in the

seventh, was continued in these isles till the
close of the tenth century of our era; but
here again theme and time and space unite
to disappoint the wish.

James III of Scotland was a true son of the
second or Italian Renaissance, as well as in
some sort a martyr to it. If ever there was a
dilettante that wore a crown, the third of our
Jameses was for sure that prince. Twenty-seven
years he reigned; so that if it be true that he
was killed by some of his subjects because he
governed the country ill (which is what our
historians allege), it should seem plain to most,
if not to them, that his assassins took a mighty
long time in which to make up their minds
touching both him and it. However, no matter
how he might rule the land, all are agreed that
James was greatly distinguished by a love of the
arts, so much so (say our historians) that to them
he gave up his days, passing hours together in
the society of the musicians, the architects,
the painters, and the men of letters that he
called to his court, and whose conversation
he preferred to that of the rude fellows who,
resenting this so reasonable preference, rose
in arms against him, and murdered him after
he was fallen from his horse.

In the lowlands of Scotland, the same tradition of culture long continued strong. In this part of the realm, the learning that came to us from Italy did much to soften manners, to lessen barbarity and check lawlessness, which (as was the case in France) the introduction of the feudal system had done much to foment, espe- cially among the nobles, and other great men of the realm. In the Gaelic-speaking parts of the kingdom, which were greatly more extensive formerly than they are now, some effects of the Renaissance in Italy took place in course of time, though later than was the case with regard to the feudal districts of the country; the cause of this being that in the highlands and the neighbour- ing isles the old tradition of learning was yet strong,[1] and the channels of impenetration less direct, less numerous, and less perfect than they were in that part of the country where the court and the seat of government were established. Still, Gaelic letters consented in

---

[1] 'Before English came among them the Gaelic nobles were wont to use Latin and Gaelic in their writings. Ruaraidh Mór, [chief of the MacLeods] was the last of the nobles in this part of the country [south-west] to observe this custom.'— Translated from the evidence of Hugh MacDonald, given before the Ossian Commission. The same witness says that the great men began to cease to entertain poets and other literary men in their households, 'about the time James succeeded to the throne of England.'

spirit at least to those of Italy when, as happened in course of time, our nobles, and even
some of their ladies, began to sing in respectable verse of shepherds and sylvan scenes and
the joys and sorrows of the pastoral life.

On the whole, then, the truth of the matter
is, that, in Scotland, old and native tradition
being joined to foreign innovation by way of
culture, there then followed this union, and
the same has been continued till late, some considerable practice of dilettanteism.   Archibald,
eighth Earl and first Marquis of Argyle, was one
who, in his time and in his day, was a notable
dilettante.   He gave much encouragement to
the poets (some of Scotland and yet others of
Ireland), who sought his society, and paid court
to his purse.   Himself wrote Gaelic verse,
though, most unfortunately, none of it appears
to have come down to us.   The Lords Stirling
and Cromarty were dilettanti also — amateurs
of the pen and lovers of the arts, though nowadays few indeed are they who care to read
what these two worthies wrote.   No doubt
figures like unto these will occur to others as
readily as, in passing to other matters, such
have occurred to me, and as yet more would
occur, I doubt, as well to others as myself,
were there any need for it, that is to say were

a whole chronicle or history of dilettanteism
in Scotland on the carpet, instead of this brief
outline of the subject, which is but intended
to serve for a kind of background to my portrait
of Lord Rosebery.

Speaking of the first Duke of Marlborough,
Bolingbroke, who extols his parts, and wonders
much at his rise to fame, says somewhere that
this was the more astonishing, and had the
greater merit, since the duke was 'a new man'
when he entered the public service of his
country, by which he means that Churchill
was not a member of one of the great families
of England, and thus he was without this powerful means to push his fortunes. The family of
Primrose is 'new' also in the same sense, since
but little had been heard of it before the year
1700, when it was ennobled in the person of
Archibald Primrose, a lawyer and a Writer to
the Signet, if I mistake not. In any event, what
is sure is, that the family of Primrose is not,
nor ever was, one of the great historic houses
of Scotland. When it first appears in story,
it was in the Whig interest; and in the same
interest, or in some one of those at least which
in course of time have come to develop out
of it, it has remained ever since apparently,
though any one less like a Whig, a Liberal,

or a Radical, and more like a Tory, a Conservative, or a Fascist, I have never set eyes on, or listened to, when public life, and the easy professions of principles that pass with many for such, were not the occasion and topic of the conversation. The family became wealthy, though it had estate enough before this good fortune happened to it, when it married into that of the late Baron Rothschild, in the person of Hannah, his daughter, who brought Lord Rosebery a large fortune. I mention these domestic details here because they are necessary to be noted, though but in brief; for dilettanteism is a flower that needs much care and every tending, punctual waterings, the richest of soils, and manures in plenty to its roots, to the end that it may be coaxed to put forth its most splendid blossom.

I think it showed some bud of promise very early in Lord Rosebery. He dilettantied into school and out of it: he dilettantied into college, from whence, still in the best dilettante mood and manner, he entered politics, with a strong bent, if not a positive aim, to communicate to his share of them at least the same spirit.

His first public employment was an under-secretaryship, an office whose duties he discharged in such a manner as might be expected

of him, that is to say with urbanity, aplomb,
and complete address. Superior scope for his
talent was afforded him when he became a
First Commissioner of Works; and yet more,
and better still, when, in the year 1886, he was
given, under Gladstone, the principal direction
of the foreign affairs of these realms.

Rosebery had a great admiration for Gladstone, and the latter was always duly sensible of
it, though I do not think that the real love
which the first had of the second, the second
entertained, in anything like the same degree
at least, for the first. My belief is, that Gladstone thought Rosebery not 'thorough' enough;
and if, earlier in his career, the former may
have come at times to suspect the sincerity of
his own devotion to Whig principles, nevertheless I think that he soon came to doubt
those of Rosebery, more often, far deeper,
and perhaps with much better cause. Gladstone admired the Scotsman's talent, was ever
forward to applaud his eloquence, and to
acknowledge with candour the value of his
services to the party; but though Rosebery
sought the society of the other, and always
professed the greatest admiration for him,
yet I thought at the time that whenever the
two happened to meet in a social way one at

least of the two was never quite at his ease. Gladstone disliked Disraeli intensely because he happened to dislike much the quality of genius that marked the other in so strong a manner; and though no doubt the able Jew and the clever Scot were two very different natures, yet hardly does the brilliance of the one light differ much in appearance—no matter how much in kind—from that of another. It was a part of Gladstone's nature to distrust others formed as Disraeli's was: and in this distrust I think that Rosebery, as being to some extent 'exotic' even as was Disraeli, shared, to this extent at least.

On the retirement of Gladstone from the premiership, which happened in the year 1894, Rosebery succeeded him. The opinion shared by many in the party at the time was that the office should have gone to Harcourt. Rosebery was sensible enough of this opinion, and knew well the strength of it among the Liberals, and in the country generally. I think that he had given way to Harcourt then as he came to give way to him afterwards, that is, willingly enough, were it not that his vanity had early proposed to him two principal ambitions, namely, to become Prime Minister of England and to win the Derby; and this I believe on the strength of a

letter which I received from him about the
time when the Harcourt quarrel was at its
height, and the whole party rife with spleen
and intrigue by consequence. He marked
the letter 'most private,' so I may not give
it even now; but this at least I may say of
it with perfect propriety, namely, that it
caused me to believe that now that his ambition
as regards the premiership was fulfilled he was
become indifferent as to whether he continued
long in it or not. Every one knows that his
administration had but a short and troubled
life: his brief reign as first minister, if it was not
inglorious, yet was little more than an episode
pour rire in the long story of party government
in England. Defeated at the elections, he
retreated to the leadership of his party, still
imagining, if not compassing, politics according
as the dilettante understands them, and is fond
to practise them, once the necessary power and
authority are his. Later, he appeared with great
to-do at Chesterfield, where, anticipating in
manœuvre our present Mr. Lloyd George, he
posed as the author and advocate of a brand
'new plan' for the Whigs. On this occasion,
however, he was but coldly received by the
Liberal chiefs; and even many of the generality
of his party, who had been well enough disposed

to him formerly, now shrank from him, wondering much within themselves what precisely he would be at.   But what my lord would be at appeared very plainly a little later on, when he sought to form a party of his own, under the denomination of the 'Liberal Imperialists.' This, I suppose, was his great stroke, his supreme essay, as regards the application of dilettante principles to English politics, in which however, as it happened, the scheme could find no soil wherein to root itself.   The squib was lit with difficulty, and burned but faintly, and in part; when at last it was brought to 'explode,' it smouldered simply, because what powder it had to it was inferior stuff, besides being damp.   In fine, the new 'party' began to disappear in the country almost as soon as it appeared in an office of its own in town; and in the year 1910 Lord Rosebery, surrendering to fate the seals of his office as patron-in-chief in Britain of political dilettanteism, retired into private life, from which he was not drawn till he was carried to the grave but a few years ago.

The snail is known by its trail almost as much as by its horns and shell.   I have no wish to compare Lord Rosebery, whom I liked, and whose talent I admired, in part at least, to a snail; but what I think on this head is, that in letters, as in politics, he was somewhat futile; in short, I think that whatever he happened to touch in either came afterwards to show unmistakable signs of the trail of the dilettante. I think, too, that if we were to take the different studies of eminent persons that he made, and that were published in book form during his lifetime, and we were to proceed to examine them, with the care which these agreeable writings demand, we might find that in them, as in the choice of subject which he made, and his mode of treatment of them generally, consists the true key to their distinguished author's mind. Hardly is it without significance that all his heroes were Tories in politics, and, farther, that themes of conquest and empire, and territorial expansion, engross his pen, and lead him to reflections and judgments little consistent, I imagine, with true Whig principles. Still, if Lord Rosebery chose, as choose he certainly did, to discover himself, in his books a Tory, but to his party and the world in general a Whig, the part of such as ponder his career and examine his public record to-day is surely to bow to the decision, leaving it to posterity and the psycho-analysts to explain the conundrum as best they may.

The writings of Lord Rosebery were a good

deal read, and admired near as much as they were read, I think, at the time; the present writer read them all as soon as each appeared, as I suppose did most people who knew him, or, not having this knowledge, yet were interested in him. Still, not every play a man goes to see he goes to see again; and so on this principle few are the books which, once read, one cares to read a second time. Rosebery's were all fragments, though fragments little comparable, I imagine, with that fragment in the shape of the beginning of a history of the revolution of 1688 which Mackintosh bequeathed to posterity—a masterpiece, though it was but a fragment. He wrote well, but then scarce might he write otherwise, having regard to his talent, and the pains he was at (at times) to improve it. He observed and studied well good models; besides, he had excellent native wit; and his knowledge and experience of 'business,' and the great world generally, helped him much when he came to treat of men—such as the two Pitts—who had been situated as he was, and who, like him, had been born into the political purple as it were.

I once asked him what model he followed, and was told that, of Englishmen, Addison pleased him most. 'A fine writer, no doubt,'

I said, 'but I prefer Dryden. It seems to me
that the other's line is somewhat too suave,
too close an imitation of the classic originals.
What the brothers Adam were to furniture,
and domestic decoration generally, Addison
is to English letters.' Still, Rosebery wrote,
as he spoke, uncommonly well: his principal
fault was that in neither one field nor the other
could he ever rise much above 'slightness,'
or appear to any greater advantage than to be
occasionally 'suggestive' in a superficial and
fleeting sort of fashion.

In fine, it seems to me that even at this distance of time his whole career and performance
in life, when submitted to the pressure of an im-
partial examination, give forth a strong aroma—
exotic and, to say truth, a trifle sickly at times
—of sham and dilettanteism. His supreme
misfortune was, I think, that almost from his
cradle he was attended by the twin spirits
of rank and fortune; and, instead of correcting,
they spoiled the child—a course which parents
and guardians too fond by nature are apt to
take. If his cradle had been poverty, his
school adversity, and his 'party' the discipline that comes of just criticism, in room of
flattery, I believe that he had come to free
himself of the trammels of dilettanteism (to

which his whole nature and breeding much inclined him); and so had come to be at last, not the disappointing man and uncertain misty figure which his memory presents to us, but something more respectable, something truer to the talent he undoubtedly had—something more worthy of the praises which some showered on him when he died.

I think that somewhat at least of the character of a true dilettante may be collected from the following lines, though I suppose that all such attempted delineations of types and natures are apt to fall short of the demands of reality, and our own demands as well in respect of them, as indeed happened to Halifax, when, in his own defence, he sought to draw the character of a trimmer:

> Pauci quos aequus amavit
> Jupiter, et ardens evenit ad aethera virtus,
> Dis genite potuere.

Still, there is a rift in the poet's lute, so far as the subject of the present sketch is concerned. He had not the even temper glanced at in the Roman lines nor yet the power to love anything deep and long, or hold to it, and know it beyond the knowledge which the effort that it cost him to gain it brought to him. He

desired and sought for himself too many of
the 'blue ribbons' of the turf of this world;
but when it happened that some of the honours
that he coveted came his way, he soon grew
tired of them. Often did he perplex and, in
perplexing, vex his friends, rejoice his enemies,
and disappoint his admirers in general, by seeming to faint when to appear as strong was essential
to his cause; by seeming to lose his better if
not his true self in dilettanteism, at seasons
and conjunctures when conduct on his part
very different to this was needed and expected
of him, and was well within his capabilities
also. Already his memory begins to 'fade,
recede, and sink,' as says St. Bede, when,
speaking of the power of the northern English
after that nation had been crushed by the arms
of Nechtan, High-King of the Picts, he thus
dismisses it from the page of history.

HISTORY AND PERSONALITY

CHAPTER IX

HISTORY AND PERSONALITY

THE difference between history proper and
biography is plain, and it is this, that
whereas the province of the first is events, that
of the second is persons. Still, the sharpness
of this distinction is lost to us, in part at least,
when we come to reflect that each of these
sciences invades at times the province of the
other, and not only invades it but treats it as
though it were its own, and therefore no ex-
clusive possession of the other. In short, he
who writes history cannot write it save he deal
in it on occasions with persons: neither can he
who writes biography write it save he come at
times to deal with events.

History proper is regarded very commonly
as the superior science of the two named; and
on this reasoning it might well be compared to
a kangaroo, which carries about with it in a
sort of pouch, formed of its own skin, its
young. Apparently, it is the more ancient
science; and, most certainly, far more history
has been written than biography. History, too,

generally speaking, is written at a greater length. Better minds and pens are drawn to its composition than are drawn, as a rule, to biography. Again, the themes of history are more important, more lofty, than such as occur to be treated of in biography, much of which is practised in a very trifling manner, and by persons, too, who are as ill qualified to it as they are, on this proof, to any one other branch of letters, and therefore literature in general.

Such in brief is the common view of it; and that there is ground, and to spare, for it, I should be loath to deny. Still, I cannot help but think that in a sense biography is a more important science than history proper, or rather, and at least, might well come to be regarded as its equal, were more care taken with the writing of it than is commonly the case, more learning and better judgment employed in it, and none but great actors chosen for it by way of subjects

Various ways or schemes of writing history have been propounded of late, and much attention, besides theory, devoted to this matter. For instance, Mr. H. A. L. Fisher has propounded of late [1] an idea of history which, if not quite as new as he, and some others, appear

[1] In his *History of Europe*, vol. i.

to think it, yet is enough so to warrant the opinion that the historians in time coming would do well to have regard to it. Shortly, his belief is that events occur in regular cycles of time; and, farther, that the authors, as it were, of these cycles are great men. This theory is broached with very considerable learning, and debated with address and skill as entirely respectable. But since I can hope with reason neither to emulate one nor to employ, in a like degree, the other, and the matter itself is extremely long: for these good reasons no detail of the arguments used can be attempted here.

But should we come, for argument's sake, to presume the substantial truth of Mr. Fisher's reasonings, in that event it is plain that we would need to revise very drastically our present notions touching the relative importance to society of history proper and biography; and even though we should come to decline to go to the great length glanced at, yet I think that what the Warden of New College says as to the subject mentioned is of a weight enough to cause us all to devote some thought to his theory, to approach it with every sign and mark of respect, and to be candid with ourselves, and him, as to what his conclusions may come to bring our own to, on the same head.

In the first case, that is, if we agree to accept Mr. Fisher out and out, as it were, in this event it is plain that biography comes at once to occupy in our regard and esteem the primacy hitherto enjoyed by history. But though this should not occur, and in the meanwhile we remain content with the second case here presumed, yet even in the lesser case we would need to have the greatest care, at least, how we approach this matter of the use and value of history proper and biography, considering one relatively to the other. He who comes to doubt, who opens his mind to reasonings contrary in form and spirit to those he has entertained formerly as to any given article of belief, is half-way gained already towards the new opinions: at least, such is my observation and such my experience.

So that, really, no matter what road we may come, or choose to take, with regard to the question mooted here, I think strongly that there is a case for a serious reconsideration at least of previous judgments and current notions with regard to it.

It was thought, and said, by some at the time that Mr. Lytton Strachey's *Life of Queen*

Victoria was new biography, that is, that the work I name discovered to us a new way of writing it. Boasts of this kind are familiar hearing nowadays; but it would be well to remember the ancient adage which affirms that there is nothing new under the sun. Essentially, this is so; and if some choose to take the developments of things, of pre-existent principles and causes, for absolute novelties, they are surely welcome to the conceit, though they should not seek to invest it with the power and authority of new found truth. Certainly, it could be proved very easily that Mr. Strachey's plan of writing the *Life of Queen Victoria* has been practised, as regards the essentials of this manner, formerly, no matter how new a turn and novel an appearance development, in the shape of the author named, may give to it.

To apply a microscope to a famous person's nature and career, and to publish the results of the experiment, or rather a series of them, is, of course, fair enough biography; and if the author not only so employs himself and science, but calls in to his aid all Vienna as well, for my part I see no just cause of complaint. Famous lives are at least susceptible to be proved the reverse; and any astronomer having a preference for the spots in the sun, as objects of study, instead of the full fair face of the luminary, and the circumadjacent phenomena of nature, is for sure privileged of his choice, and, conceivably, may do a real service to society, as well as his profession and himself.

At the same time, it must be allowed very freely that the psycho-analytic mode or method of writing biography tends to breed in him that practises it, and demonstrably in his writings, a spirit of over-emphasis, of conjecture and speculation (considered as such only) and bold exaggeration. I do not affirm that these blemishes mark Mr. Strachey's work, though I am well aware that some have charged him with them, and written even other lives and accounts in order to correct what they think subject to correction in Mr. Strachey, and, therefore, ought to be corrected. But what I do affirm, and think a common opinion, is, that biography, planned on psycho-analytic lines, is often great rubbish, and farther mischievous rodomontade, considering it in a point of view of the probabilities of natures and events. Without a doubt, biography takes on this character, where it has it, owing to the extreme uncertainty of even the first principles of the science to which these writers trust in order to explain their subjects to their readers, and sell their books; but, at

the same time, I cannot help but think that
themselves also are just objects of suspicion: in
fine, false, or at least science that is but precariously established, and a disordered imagination co-operate in ill works very often,
the first stimulating the second to sallies of absurdity greater even than those that are natural
to it; sallies, too, which it would not practise,
very probably, were it not for this stimulant,
and its own strong genius of reaction to it.

The grand object of history is truth; and
the 'problem' of it to discover truth. History resembles a vast moor, about which mist
rolls perpetually. Here and there, the mist is
'patchy,' so that objects can be seen through
it with a fair certainty; but, for the most part,
it is exceeding dense, hiding everything from
view. For the most part, too, this moor is
trackless; and huge boulders, mosses, holes
and caverns in the earth, deep streams and
rivers mark its surface.

The part as the task of the historian is to
explore, and map, this waste; but such written
plan as he has to guide him in both is but
fragments often, and often, too, fragments
very obscure as to the true sense of them.
Ever he must trust to his eyes, and use his
judgment; but then his burden is not lightened

for him by reason of the fact that, even as he goes forward from his starting-point, the mist about him thickens, and paths and tracks grow yet more scarce and insecure. In Dodgson's *Hunting of the Snark*, the Bellman and his fellow-undertakers are represented as pursuing it with 'forks and hope'; but it should seem that the Germans have improved somewhat on this method by pursuing truth in history with the appendix and the footnote. But it appears, too, that in some this form of venery excites, not admiration, but rather irritation of mind, mixed with some contempt of those who use it. For instance, Dr. Rice Holmes is one who has written strongly in this sense, in a passage of the preface to the first edition of his *Caesar's Conquest of Gaul*, a passage which I am about to quote in full in this place, since it contains some censure of Germanic super-industry in verbosity which I think both just and seasonable:

It is to be wished rather than hoped [says he] that the appalling mass of printed matter which, for four centuries, has been accumulating round the *Commentaries*, may not be swelled in the future by mere verbiage. If only the editors of German periodicals would restrain the ardour of the emendators who inundate them with futile conjectures, they would be setting a good

example. The *Tabula Conjecturorum* which Meusel prints
at the end of his great *Lexicon Caesarianum* fills thirty-
six pages super royal octavo, closely printed in double
columns; and of all these conjectures those which
really deserve the name of emendations would not fill
a single page, while those which have been unanimously
adopted might be counted upon the fingers of one hand.
In the Greek state of Locri there was a rule that whoever
proposed a new law should do so with a rope round his
neck; and, if his proposal were rejected, should be
strangled on the spot. It would be a good thing if
editors would combine to deal with emendators in a
like spirit.

And for my part I think that if the same proposed
rule could be extended so as to embrace footnote writers whose *notanda* are not such strictly,
but vast extensions of previous sermonizings,
together with all perpetrators of excessive
'documentation,' a riddance to written history
would thereby be effected on account of which
the relief experienced would be profound and
general both.

'Every man in his own humour,' was said
formerly, and might be said yet; and on this
principle, let every one that has a mind and
talent to it enjoy, and practise, his own way
of writing history proper and biography. It
matters little in the long run, I imagine, whether,

with regard to the first, our approach to it be through Spengler or Fisher, or, with regard to the second, we fall in with Plutarch or pitch camp with Strachey. In fine, it is not the method that counts, that should prevail with us; but the matter, that is the written effects of the historian's or the biographer's industry. Bodin ascribed race to differences of climates; and Ridgeway thought that those of physiognomy in man are due to variations of temperature; and though I should be reluctant to follow either of these sages in either conjecture, yet I have more respect for M. Henri Hubert, who, in his great work on the Celts in Europe, gives it as his opinion that the French excellence in respect of history and memoir-writing springs from the first historic inhabitants of France, the Gauls, whose descendants were long our friends and allies in peace and war.

Still, where questions of particular aptitudes, and the excellence that is bred of them, are concerned, we should do well, I think, always to walk warily, remembering ever the extreme uncertainty of this matter of race, and, further, that our first sure views of society in the west of Europe discover to us already 'a strange medley of races,' and therefore but slender ground on which to build up theories of the nature indulged by this ingenious M. Hubert, and others.

However, I am much of the opinion that the French technique as regards the art of writing generally bears a strong resemblance to that which was practised by the Celts, and is used still—though probably unconsciously—by such followers of this Muse in these isles as still use a Celtic tongue, instead of English language, in their writings, and who, in the province mentioned, are worthy to be compared with the French. But then here opens to us so large and perplexed a topic, no matter whether we have regard to it in its old or in its modern aspect, or yet more philosophically, in its entirety, and therefore not in part, that I must needs decline to pursue it any farther in this place, but, instead, seek to draw these observations to some sort of head.

Excluding then, so far as the present work is concerned, all debate of excellence, of merit relatively to peoples, persons, and things, we are led to the conclusion that the French practised the writing of history and memoirs a good deal earlier than the English, than the Germanic peoples generally practised either one or other or both. If we except St. Bede, we will need to take a big leap down in English

history before we come to a flowering of letters
in respect of the two sciences glanced at,
that is in any way justly comparable with
that of the French in the same period. There
is no question but that early French literature
is much richer in histories and memoirs than
English; and this early and common turning of
the French mind towards the subjects spoken of,
I have no hesitation in ascribing to yet earlier
Celtic example. The principal families among
the Celts of these isles, following the practice of the nobles of contemporary Gaul, were
long used to entertain in their service historians, poets, and reciters of tales, fragments
(in considerable number) of whose works have
descended to us, but the vast bulk of which is
now perished, though vouched for by tradition
that is entirely respectable. Giving evidence
at the public inquiry into the authenticity of
the Ossianic writings that took place in Scotland not long after the controversy touching
them arose, Hugh MacDonald (a native of the
Isles, and one of several witnesses called on
the occasion mentioned) testified that in former
times the Gaelic nobles were used to protect
and reward the historians, and other literary
men, in their midst, till about the time of the
succession of James VI to the English throne,

when (says he) they began to discourage and
cast them off, leaving them to shift for themselves.   I mention Hugh here, not because the
testimony which he gives is singular, and therefore cannot be supported by other of the same
kind (which is far indeed from being the case),
but because it fixes the time at or about which
the great cultural change to which he refers
began to take place.

I believe, too, that, speaking generally, the
Celtic and the French way of approach to
history (subjectively considered), their mode or
manner of writing it, and their notions as to
its proper ends and uses, are the same, though
in what this sameness consists is not to be set
forth here at any great length, but, on the contrary, must be touched but lightly, and, even in
this slight manner, but so much as is necessary,
in order to afford some illustration to the
present theme.

The Celtic genius, applied to history, sees
in it persons, rather than events and things.
Though it is not entirely indifferent, of course,
to the second and third, yet it is true to say
that it ever lays a deal more emphasis on the
first.   In other words, the strong individuality
of this genius leads it to conceive of history as
the science of setting forth in narrative form the

story of a succession of natures that are more
the arbiters than the sport of events; but
then to this tendency to enlarge in narrative
on persons, in contradistinction to the circumstances which, according to the opinion of
other peoples, are the causes rather than the
effects of such natures, we find associated yet
another quality; and this also must be dealt with
very briefly.

Such observers of old as mention in their
writings the Celts agree in saying that the
common mind of this people inclined them much
to the use of enigma in their writings. In
short, it ever pleased them to weave a strong
thread of fable through all their narrative;
and if any one, reading them, should fail to
collect, from what they had written, that which
was in their mind at the time—this seems to
have caused them but small concern, so long
as they were clear to minds better initiated
in the mysteries of their manner, and their
craft according as they practised it. Again,
in their writings, the Celts of old avoided the
use of long chains of deductions and concatena-
tions of reasonings: instead, they equipped
their narrative much as we equip our roads,
with signposts set at convenient points, that
direct to ways down which the traveller may

pass if he has a mind to wander from the main
road, or some occasion of moment calls him off
it, and thus into one or other of these by-ways.
All these mannerisms of letters were accom-
modated to a style of composition which may
be seen to advantage in the Irish Annals, where
it appears, though in a much condensed and
abbreviated form, agreeably to the genius of
the chronicle, which, unlike history proper,
consists of brief informations set forth with as
few words as possible, and not much improved
by the writer's art. However, in such fragments of the larger pieces as have come down
to us, and that have been transcribed and
translated, and published within recent years,
and particularly, perhaps, in the narratives of
an historical nature of which our epic poetry
consists in part: in these sources, I say, the
nature, as the quality, of the style used for
history is sufficiently illustrated; and I leave it
to the curious generally to compare it with that
practised in France in early times by such as
there turned their minds and hands to the
branch of letters spoken of.

The emphasis that was laid on personality
by the Celts and the weight given to it in such
history as they uttered, render it very probable
that had their culture survived, in a degree

proportionate to its early importance, the shocks, rubs, and interruptions given it by the intrusion into these isles of the feudal style of rule and mode or way of social life, it had continued to develop in the same direction; and this doubtless (had it come to pass) would have pleased Mr. Fisher, and others, who attach far more importance to the workings of personality in history than they do to those of institutions and events, which they think explain history to us not near as well as the other does so. Presuming, then, the occurrence of this probability, yet another, as plausible as the other, is, that history proper and biography, as practised by the Celts, had come, in course of time, to take on a quasi-synthetic character, to be, in other words, a kind of blend of all the previously enacted personalities of history, age after age and generation after generation of historians and biographers coming to use the compound so obtained in order to explain to themselves and others the main phenomena of both.

It is plain that in a true synthesis, the different elements of which it is made up are preserved intact, whole and separate, in the union of forces or 'values' that is the consequence, the true professed end, of this process, *qua* process; whereas, in a blend, these formative elements are lost, their respective identities being as it were a forfeit to the mingling that must take place in order to effect this, or any other, blend or mixture. Thus, in synthetic history, as in biography of the same character, the capital means to all the explanatory ends of both would be personality in the gross, and yet, at the same time, differentiated personality. As regards this sort of 'enigma' the Celts should excel: the French have made some progress in it already; but, on the other hand, our neighbours across the Border, some of whose sons of Homer have this word 'synthesis' much on the tip of their pens at the moment, appear to have made little or none, as yet, towards the implementing their professed desires in this respect.

If we must specialize in history, or rather as regards the manner of writing it, it behoves us to take good heed that our choice of a medium is sound, better constituted, and less precariously established, than some at least have been that were recommended formerly with all the vehemence of fashion, and the heat of a craze of the hour; but now are not—as, for instance, the application of philosophy to history, which at one time was thought to be every historian's philosopher's stone, but now is discarded. Apparently, before some could discover that history, properly conceived and executed, is of itself philosophy in plenty, that philosophy runs all through it, and informs its different parts, some time was needed, and understanding not yet discovered necessary to be had, in order to persuade these zealots of a craze that their pet specific was absurd, that history is one thing, and philosophy, as practised by the philosophers, is science quite different; and, consequently, that to apply to one the methods, the machinery, of the other is but to make a fool of both in the public gaze, and, from first to last, is entirely unworkable.

These observations are very just, I think, with regard to synthetical methods in history also, of which we hear a deal nowadays, and which some cry up as though they were a specific sent from the gods to men. Some colour at least is given to the latter notion by reason of the temper of the times touching the article of religion; for are we not told to worship, not one God, but several? to seek for foundations in respect of religious faith, not where near two thousand years of Christianity have concurred to set them, but rather anywhere else; but preferably amidst the ruins of paganism, or

in the ethic swamps and marshes, the arid wastes
and sandy deserts of pantheism? And this at
least we may affirm with perfect truth, namely,
that all this exhortation now transacting among
us, the object of which is to persuade such as
write history to write it on a synthetic plan,
bears a very suspicious resemblance to the
current pantheism, as well in matters of state,
in government, and civil rule generally, as in
those of the spirit, and the religious conscience
and experience of man.

But then if any one, having digested Spin-
oza, ransacked Leibnitz, and thought long on
the late Mr. Victor Branford, should come to
transact, or at least to essay, a series of history
conceived on a synthetic plan, where and
how should he begin his labours; and, pray,
where and how should he bring them, and his
synthesis, to an end? History is a harmony of
continuous action in terms, and in the form, of
drama, the essential principle of which is laid,
not in formalism, but in the full and free associa-
tion in time and space of conjuncture and the
human ethos; and for this reason to oblige it
to any particular mode or form, to tie it up
or down to any one 'school' in preference
to another or the rest, would defeat in the
event its true end and real purpose, would so

interrupt the natural flow of it from time, as we know and reckon it, towards eternity as to make of it in the event, not story more or less credible, more or less connected, and more or less plain to understanding, but a bewildering, and intractable, pastiche of disjointed fact and roaming fancy — not a series of representations, well managed and continuously plausible, such as the best theatre offers to us to some extent, but a succession of 'pictures,' abruptly presented, crudely articulated, mechanically differentiated, enlarged to absurdity here, and reduced to wellnigh imperceivable smallness there—for no discoverable reason whatever apparently—and therefore comparable in some sort to those impostures on art, on verisimilitude, nature, unity, and good taste which in the garish and draughty halls devoted to the display of such objects pass with the multitude for entertainment, and, it may be, in exceptionally imbecile cases, for instruction also.

Farther, it is of the nature of the synthesis that it cannot be bent, or stayed, or deflected to purpose, once it has been 'released,' started on a course; so that he who so embarks his intellectual fortunes embarks them at his peril, that is, knowing nothing whatever as to whither

his adventure may take him, or what disservice
this force uncontrolled may do him and his
cause on the uncharted seas that roll before
him. Such a man, be he poet, be he dramatist
or historian, resembles one who should stand
by the banks of a great river in flood, and who
sees, as there he stands—borne swiftly by him
on the swollen bosom of the waters, and half
submerged — the corpses of men and other
creatures that have perished in the deluge,
the wreckage of homesteads, and much other
flotsam and jetsam of catastrophe by tempest.
For this is history; and such, too, is the historian.
Is not the first powerless as a gnat to control
the forces of nature that the storm has loosed,
and the second as incapable to weave of the
hurrying wave that sweeps this derelict matter
along with it seawards — what? — a trivial
thread of doubtful synthesis in history! How
entirely extravagant, and completely unworkable, theory may appear, and zeal misdirect
itself, as well as others, Mr. John Middleton
Murry proves in a writing of his, published
no great while ago, on the subject of literary
criticism. This writer also is a synthesist; and
so, in order to improve the state of modern
criticism, what he proposes is, that an 'hierarchy
of Prototypes' should be formed to take charge

and dictate to it, consisting, he suggests, of the
First Person of the Holy Trinity, Shakespeare,
Keats, Goethe, Melville, Dostoevsky, and
Tchekov.   Surely, it is here the best charity to
think that rather was it a passing intoxication,
begot of a more than commonly heady kind of
theory, than sober intention, or grave reality,
that has blown these fumes into this honest
critic's head.

The chase whose end is to fix history in
'science' goes on always.   Theory of it after
theory of it appears; but who shall say with
truth that any of these appearances has occurred
to much effect heretofore?   Is not history of itself science enough already, without our seeking
continuously to make it so in the narrow sense
of the word to which the cant and usage of
the hour are fond to restrict it?   In the world
of the polite sciences and the arts, as in that
of politics and social endeavour, are Utopias
also; and of these perhaps the oldest, considering it as an object of man's quest, the most
sought for, and surely the hardest to find, is
'Fixed Principles,' a land of mystery evidently,
girt with rock and raging sea, remote as the
uttermost parts of the universe, shrouded in
mist that never lifts and elusive as air to the
curious mariner.   Apparently, the lot of man

in this life is to be bantered continuously by
the prescriptions of the fate which himself, in
the shape of his own greed and want of per-
spicacity, has drawn down on him from on
high; thus, with unflagging zeal, and ever
sanguine mind, he seeks perfection where none
is, nor, by the nature of himself and his im-
mediates, can be; fixity where is naught but
the shifting sands of rolling deserts; and a
happy issue to all his cherished undertakings
where to indulge the hope is plainly but silly
snare and gross delusion.

In fine, though personality should come to
occupy the place in history which it enjoyed
in the Celtic schools, before they were dissipated; and events and institutions, considered
as *materia historica*, come to be reduced, in
the scheme of it, even as they were reduced
in the ancient seats of learning spoken of;
though history proper, and all biography,
should come to be written as one long-laboured
synthesis, or whole cycles of events, or the
rise and fall of particular cultures usurp the
room of the criteria now in use among us—
in these events, 'fixed principles' would yet
be wanting to history, and its message to man
would be no more sure, no more 'science,'
in a positive sense, than it is at present, or

has been so in all time past. The changes glanced at would not signify in reality more than so many changes of method; and though these particular readjustments as regards the historian's way of approach to the object of his studies might be the means of introducing some improvements into the written effects of them, yet ever there would be to reckon loss as well as gain; for like the tide, which is his, and its, true type and symbol, all progress on man's part towards perfection, and a phantom security of tenure in respect of it, is but as ebb and flow, flow and ebb; and the sea's unchanging uncertainty but the mirror of his own in this world.